St. Theresa
the Little Flower

By
Sr. Gesualda of the Holy Spirit

Translated by
Margaret M. Repton

ST. PAUL BOOKS & MEDIA

NIHIL OBSTAT:
Arthur J. Scanlan, S.T.D.
Censor Librorum

IMPRIMATUR:
+ Patrick Cardinal Hayes

Library of Congress Cataloging-in-Publication Data

Jesualde of the Holy Spirit, Sister.
    [Sainte Thérèse de l 'Enfant Jesus. English]
    St. Theresa, the Little Flower / by Sr. Gesualda of the Holy
Spirit ; translated from the French by Margaret M. Repton.
       p. cm.
    Translation of: Sainte Thérèse de l'Efant Jesus.
    ISBN 0-8198-6817-5
    1. Thérèse, de Lisieux, Saint, 1873-1897. 2. Christian saints—
France—Lisieux—Biography. 3. Lisieux (France)—Biography.
I. Title. II. Title: Saint Theresa, the Little Flower.
Bx4700.T5J4513 1991
282'.092—dc20
[B]   91-35912
                         CIP

St. Paul Books & Media is the publishing house of the Daughers of
St. Paul, an international congregation of women religious serving the
Church with the communications media.

1   2   3   4   5   6   7   8   9   98   97   96   95   94   93   92   91

Contents

Dawn Veiled in Mourning

Until a few years ago, who had ever heard of Lisieux? Its name was practically unknown and was of little interest to anyone, including those already on French soil.

It was a humble little Norman town; a mere handful of houses with penthouse roofs dominated on one side by a tall belfry, and on the other by an imposing Gothic Cathedral. It had no importance of its own then, and gave no indication of its future renown. It would not be a glory such as the world gives, but it would come from a humble young nun whose name God was pleased to exalt after death, because in life she had been most self-effacing.

In our day this obscure little country town is known to all the world. It has become a center on which converge pilgrims of every nation. They do not go there for pleasure or out of curiosity; they go to kneel beside the tomb wherein for some years had lain the mortal remains of St. Theresa of the Child Jesus, to see the humble convent where she spent her days, and to visit the beautiful shrine where her precious remains had reposed since she was raised to the honors of the altar.

Born in Alençon on January 2, 1873, she came to Lisieux at the age of four and a half years, and died there in her twenty-fourth year, on September 30, 1897.

In September, 1877, when she first set foot in Lisieux, she was dressed in black. The somberness of her attire strongly accentuated the golden glints of her fair curly hair, and gave to her sad, forlorn little face the look of an angel. What sympathy, what pity did she not inspire in all who saw her; so pretty, so very young, in deep mourning!

What happened to her was one of the worst misfortunes that can befall a child: the loss of the one person on earth most necessary, her mother. She was a mother still young, active, energetic and good, a truly Christian soul, profoundly pious; a woman devoted to God and her family. She awaited with joy the birth of each child, seeing in them a heavenly blessing. Then she guarded her children with love, and educated them in the Catholic faith. She seemed indispensable, but in the words of Isaiah: "The ways of God are not our ways, nor is the mind of God like unto ours"; and so, on August 28, 1877, God took her to himself. She left a grief-stricken husband and five daughters, the eldest seventeen and the youngest four and a half.

The anguish of the deathbed scene was so indelibly impressed on the mind of the youngest child, our little Theresa, that for the rest of her life she would recall it vividly: her mother receiving Viaticum, her father weeping during the administering of the Sacrament of the Anointing of the Sick, and her sisters praying fervently. Although Theresa was so very young, she witnessed the whole of this scene without a tear, and realized from that moment the futility of earthly happiness and the reality of eternal joys.

The funeral over, the five girls, dumb with sorrow, gazed at each other, their eyes swollen with grief and tears. The old family servant, looking at the children exclaimed: "My poor little ones! You no longer have a mother." Then Celine, with an impulse of warm affection, threw herself into the arms of her older sister Marie-Louise, saying:

"Well, you shall be my mother." Theresa, however, who invariably imitated her, refrained from doing so this time. She looked with great tenderness at Pauline, the second sister, and went and hid her face on her shoulder, and very timidly whispered: "For me, my mother will be Pauline." However, from that day a cloud obscured the happiness of little Theresa. She became shy and sensitive, and did not outgrow this until she was almost fourteen.

The First Grace

The first grace that God conferred on our saint was the good fortune of being born into a family that practiced all the virtues of Catholicity.

It is easy to trace the finger of God in the singular way in which the parents of Theresa met. When Louis Martin was but twenty, in the year 1843, he felt drawn to the Order of Monks of the great St. Bernard. Picturing in his mind the pure white snow and profound silence, so conducive to contemplation, he seemed to hear the cries of the poor lost travelers on their journey across the Alps, some of them dying of intense cold. He felt a longing to give his life to their service. What an attraction on the mountain slopes so far from the world and yet full of solicitude for his neighbor!

He wended his way to the monastery and rang the bell. The venerable prior who interviewed him was agreeably struck with the appearance and manner of the young man, whom he found to his surprise was not a tourist seeking his way, but one desiring to embrace the monastic life and retire from the world.

"Have you passed all your Latin examinations?" the prior asked. As Louis answered in the negative, the prior continued: "I am sorry, my son, but that is one of the entrance requirements. Do not be discouraged, however. Go back and study hard and then perhaps when you come again I may receive you with open arms."

Rather downhearted, our would-be monk retraced his steps, feeling like an exile. But time changed his feelings; the monastic life became only a beautiful dream, as he realized that God had other designs for his future.

A few years later, in the town of Alençon, a young girl named Marie Zelie Guerin, whose countenance shone with zeal and good will, accompanied by her mother, presented herself at the convent of the Sisters of St. Vincent de Paul and asked for admission; she wished to give her life, under the white coif of the Sisters of Charity, to nursing the sick in the infirmary wards.

The Reverend Mother Superior, a woman of great insight, inspired by the Holy Spirit, told her quite frankly that she felt she did not have a vocation to the religious life; that no doubt God had different plans for her, and perhaps she would be instrumental in bringing souls to God in quite another way.

St. Joseph Helps

The members of two families, Martin and Guerin, although living in the same town of Alençon, had never met, until one day Zelie, while crossing the St. Leonard bridge, carelessly walked into a young man coming from the opposite direction. To add to her confusion, while apologizing, she noticed he was young and good looking. Perhaps it was but natural that from that moment she began to think of him somewhat romantically. It seemed to her as if this must be the answer to her secret and fervent prayers. She had asked God, since she was unable to enter the religious life, to grant her the grace to marry and have many children so that she might dedicate them all to him. Therefore, she prayed for a good Catholic husband.

After a short courtship, Louis and Zelie were married on July 13, 1858, in the Church of Our Lady in Alençon.

Louis did not know of his bride's desire to have many children and had ideas of practicing continence in his Christian marriage. He broached the subject on their wedding night. She obediently consented, although it destroyed all her dearest hopes.

After a year, however, he realized the sacrifice he was asking of his wife and he subjected his wish to hers.

Nine children were born to them, four of whom died in

infancy, while the five lived to consecrate their lives to God.

Their names were as follows, in the order of their birth: Marie-Louise, Marie-Pauline, Marie-Leonie, Marie-Helen (died aged four), Marie-Joseph-Louis, Marie-Joseph-John-Baptist, Marie-Celine, Marie-Melanie-Theresa (died aged three months), and Marie-Frances-Theresa. The two boys bearing the name of St. Joseph were born after many prayers for sons to be priests and missionaries; but God's ways are not our ways, and one little Joseph came and soon went to heaven; another arrived, and he, too, after a very short stay went to join his brother. After that the Martins were resigned, and no longer petitioned God for a missionary. If they could have looked into the future, what intense joy would have pervaded their souls, for it has been written about their youngest child: "Theresa is a veritable little missionary; her words are forcible, irresistible, and always to the point. Her whole life has a charm of its own that she will never lose, and any soul abandoning itself to her teaching will never suffer from tepidity or fall into the meshes of sin."

Did not her own parents become missionaries? For the first edition of the Portuguese translation of the *Story of a Soul*, the Reverend Father Santana, S.J., wrote this dedication:

"To the saintly and immortal memory of Louis-Joseph-Stanislaus Martin and his wife Marie-Zelie Guerin, blessed parents of St. Theresa of the Child Jesus, who serve as an example to all Christian parents. They had no idea of this great future apostolate, but unknown even to themselves they paved the way for it by the perfection of their lives."

Many were their trials, but a holy resignation was their attitude toward God who, as an ever loving Father, never abandons his little ones.

The dawn of each day found them at his altar; they knelt together at the Eucharistic table. They observed most rigorously all the precepts of the Church. They invariably prayed together, following the example of M. Martin's old father, Captain Martin, whom no one, they said, could listen to reciting the Lord's Prayer and remain unmoved.

Mme. Martin used to say, "People are subject to illusions" and, "If they possess riches, they at once crave for honors, and when these are obtained they become even more discontent, not realizing that the human heart is created to be satisfied by God alone." All her maternal ambitions were directed toward heaven; the world and its ways had no place in her heart.

"Four of my dear children," she would say, "are where I would wish them; the others will join them some day, laden with more merits, because they will have fought the more."

In consoling her sister-in-law, Mme. Guerin, over the loss of her newborn baby, she revealed her innermost thoughts under a similar trial. "When I closed the eyes of my dear ones, I felt a great sorrow in my soul, but at the same time I was resigned. I have never for a moment regretted what I suffered for them.

"I have heard others say: 'It would have been better had they not been born at all,' but I would not let them entertain such thoughts. We cannot put a few physical pains in the balance against the eternal happiness of our children. They are not lost forever...I shall meet them one day in heaven."

The priest-missionary of the Martin household was not a son, but a daughter, a gentle creature who was to rise to great heights in conquering souls for heaven and for the missionary field. Like Theresa, her sisters all consecrated themselves to God, thus completing their mother's offering of them to God.

Four of them entered the Carmel at Lisieux: Marie Louise (Sister Marie of the Sacred Heart); Marie Pauline (Sister Agnes of Jesus); Marie Celine (Sister Genevieve of the

Holy Face); Marie Frances Theresa (Sister Theresa of the Child Jesus). Marie Leonie entered the Visitation Convent at Le Mans.

It would seem as if that first year of sacrifice on the part of the parents had brought great grace upon them and their children.

The little missionary, Theresa, was born on January 2, 1873. She was baptized on the fourth, having had to wait for her godfather to arrive at Alençon. Those two days were a time of great anxiety for the poor mother, who dreaded the risk of the child's dying without Baptism.

At the sacred font she received the name of Marie Frances Theresa. She was generally called by the last, and often by the French diminutive "Theresine." That is why to her family, as well as to outsiders, she still goes by her own favorite name of "little Theresa" or "the dear little saint."

This idea of "littleness" was an integral part of her life and accompanied her even to the glory of eternity. To one who inquired of her what name she should call her by should she meet her in heaven, she replied: "Call me Theresine."

The mother desired to nurse Theresa, but after a few weeks found she was no longer able to do so and wondered if, again, she was going to lose one of her dearly loved babies.

The doctor advised a wet nurse, a strong healthy country woman, who would put new life into the child.

The next morning at dawn Mme. Martin started off on the road to Semalle, about five miles from Alençon, to see a peasant woman whom she had employed before and who was then nursing a baby of her own.

On her return she found her little Theresa livid and cold. "I am too late," she thought in anguish, and the wet nurse echoed, "Too late!"

The poor mother, her heart torn with sorrow, still clung to one hope. She ran into her room and fell on her knees before the statue of St. Joseph, and with sobs and tears besought him to obtain for her a miracle. She asked this with full confidence in God's power and mercy. Then she went back to look at the baby, and great was her joy to behold the blessed infant taking nourishment and, it seemed, holding on to life. The improvement was only temporary, however, for after a few minutes Theresa suffered a relapse.

Mme. Martin was one of those strong souls cast in a heroic mold, and in her great faith and love she found strength to say with bowed head: "The Lord has given and the Lord has taken away. Blessed be the name of the Lord." This was apparently what God was waiting for before granting the hoped-for miracle.

No sooner were her words of resignation to the divine will uttered, than the infant opened her eyes and smiled at her mother.

St. Joseph, special protector of Carmel, saved for Carmel this delicate flower.

A week later the wet nurse returned to her home in the country, taking with her her little foster child in the hope that there she might grow strong. Theresa remained with her about a year.

The Martin Fireside

The Martin family lived in comfort. They had worked hard to obtain it, and their labors had been blessed by God because they always endeavored to do his holy will.

M. Martin had a fine goldsmith's establishment and his wife had a successful lace business making the famous "point d'Alençon."

After having been refused entry into the Convent of the Visitandines, Zelie realized she might marry and took this means of earning enough money for her "dot" (dowry), so as not to have to be dependent on her husband's family.

She could not expect much from her father, who was a retired military man and who had her brother, Isadore, and her younger sister to provide for, so she had every reason to wish to provide for herself. Before deciding, however, she turned with ardent prayer to our Blessed Mother Mary, asking her for light and counsel.

One day, the 8th of December to be exact, the feast of the Immaculate Conception, Zelie was suddenly struck by an inner voice saying almost like a command: "Make point d'Alençon lace."

This was not a foolish illusion; she took it to be a direct reply from our Lady.

17

Without wasting any time, and with her wonderful and unfailing energy, she set herself to learning the various processes necessary for making this beautiful lace. She specialized in making small pieces which were to be put together afterwards. She interested a certain number of workers, with herself at the head, and carried on the work even after her marriage. The business flourished to such a degree that in 1870, M. Martin gave up his goldsmith's shop and came to the aid of his wife. He traveled for her with samples of lace, and kept the accounts.

The secret of their success? It is this, in a nutshell: the day of rest was most rigorously kept. On the day of the Lord and all feast days the Martin shop was closed to all customers. Materially it was a loss, of course, not only because in those days the laws concerning closing were very lax and people did as they pleased, but Sunday was the very day when all the young girls from the country came into town to make their purchases, especially if there was a wedding in view. Some of M. Martin's friends counseled him to do as others; that is, to put the shutters up in the front of the shop for the sake of appearance, but leave the side door open for the customers; thus neither his good name nor his purse would suffer. But a good Catholic is never a pharisee, and M. Martin energetically opposed such a double-faced proceeding. He made a dignified refusal and went on his own way, telling his evil counselors he preferred God's blessings to any earthly gain.

The Eucharistic Sacrifice was for this Christian couple the sun that illumined the dawn of every day. Each morning, they attended early Mass. Frequently they received Holy Communion. On their return home they assembled the entire household for morning prayers. In the course of the day they encouraged each other by reading aloud from the lives of the saints. A visit to the Blessed Sacrament in one church or another was the object of their afternoon walk. Night prayers by the assembled family preceded their repose. Each evening, therefore, the angels were able to carry a fresh message of fealty and love to the throne of God.

As love of one's neighbor is simply a manifestation of the love of God, it could not help but inflame the heart of Louis Martin; in him certainly reigned justice and charity. He forbade the running of any credits and insisted on cash payment for all goods he purchased. He never allowed the workmen's wages to be in arrears, and never retained unjustly any sum due them. He was also very strict with himself by never allowing expenditures to exceed his income. His charity was spontaneous and generous, and he never let human respect deter him from the performance of it.

Coming across a poor epileptic at the station one day, who, besides looking half-starved had not the wherewithal to purchase a ticket to his destination, M. Martin took off his own hat, put an offering in it, and invited all the bystanders to follow his example until he had collected a sufficient amount to pay the man's railway fare. The recipient was moved to tears by this unexpected act of kindness.

Another time, seeing a drunken man lying in a ditch by the roadside, M. Martin picked him up, dusted him, and offering his arm helped him home as if it were the most natural thing in the world.

For a pastime he occasionally went fishing, and he always gave the fish he caught to the Poor Clares, who were most grateful.

Mme. Martin was not far behind her husband in acts of charity. For weeks she sat up day and night with a poor servant girl who was ill, and procured for her all the medicine and dainties that a fond mother could have thought of for her child, and which were entirely beyond the means of the girl's parents. Another time she was brought into court for taking a child away from its guardians—two old women who were treating the poor little one unmercifully while being paid to care for her.

Louis and Zelie Martin both came from military stock, their parents having fought in the war of the Empire and for its restoration. With love of God and neighbor they also had great love and enthusiasm for France—a very laudable virtue.

In 1870, at the time of the Franco-Prussian war, Zelie wrote: "It may be that the men from forty to fifty years of age will be called. I am daily expecting the news; my husband does not dread it; in fact he often tells me that had he been a little younger he would have been off long ago among the French sharpshooters."

She would not admit that anyone could be so unpatriotic as to hold back when one's country is in peril and one's brothers are laying down their lives on the battlefield.

"How could anyone do such a thing?" she exclaimed with noble disdain, when told of a lady who had succeeded in hiding her husband during the mobilization.

When the Prussians invaded Alençon she had nine of the rank and file quartered in her house. They destroyed all her beautiful order and reduced the whole place to a pitiable state; but she was never heard to murmur and kept her peace of soul through it all.

A woman so upright, courageous, energetic, and at the same time so full of ineffable tenderness, must necessarily have inspired her daughters with a great sense of duty and love of sacrifice. Life is not a dream but a reality, based on love and sacrifice.

Life has few roses and many thorns; few smiles and many tears. Therefore, this good mother brought up her daughters from their earliest childhood not to heed the pinpricks but to bear sorrow with courage, to live with their eyes and hearts uplifted to heaven, ever working for supernatural motives...according to that saying of Blessed Frances of Amboise, almost a prototype of Mme. Martin:

"In everything seek first the love of God; let him be loved in your joys and above all, let him be loved in your sorrows."

We will give an example:

While still very young, Marie Louise, the eldest child, was obliged to undergo a slight operation on her teeth. She was told to suffer it without complaining and to offer the pain for the soul of her grandfather in case he should still be in purgatory. This was sufficient to give the child courage, and the dentist marveled at her fortitude.

On looking at her teeth again, however, he decided against operating and Marie, very much upset, said to her mother: "O Mother, what a pity; poor dear grandpapa would have been released from purgatory."

It was always thus. Zelie knew how to influence their will with her affectionate persuasion, giving them that powerful impulse that encouraged them not merely to accept the sacrifice with resignation but to desire it with a generous abnegation; not a languid acceptance of what cannot be avoided, but a loving and ardent fulfilling of a duty. After all, she had asked her child to suffer pain without complaining to release a soul from purgatory, but the child had been even more generous.

Soon after her grandfather's death Zelie wrote: "If God so willed it, I would pledge myself at once to bear all his purgatory and mine. Suffering causes me no fear. To suffer seems to me the most natural thing in the world, and I should be so glad to know of his happiness."

Thus did she generously offer herself for him! Her words were not idle ones, either. No sacrifice, however great, had ever deterred her, no trial had ever broken her spirit.

"What a noble soul!" said Mme. Martin's elder sister, a nun of great sanctity at the Visitation Convent at Le Mans. This holy nun did much to encourage her sister Zelie in all the virtues. In a letter to her written on the death of little Marie Helene she says: "I cannot think of you as anything but fortunate to give to heaven elect souls who will be your joy in the hereafter. Then your faith and your trust which have never wavered will one day reap a magnificent reward. Be sure that our Lord will bless you."

God was, indeed, well pleased with her and gave her the great saint she craved for so long; this was the little girl we left with her wet nurse in the country at Semalle.

The Return Home

Theresa, the little wild flower of the fields, returned on the second of April, in the year 1874, to be a little hothouse plant. She came home to be sheltered by her mother.

Like all babies placed out to nurse, she had become quite a little peasant child, running wild in the fields and giving all her affection to her adopted mother and family with never a thought of her own relatives, whom she did not know, as she had left them at such a tender age.

Therefore, when the wet nurse went to do some necessary shopping and left Theresa with her own mother she began to cry. At her wit's end one day, when Rosina the nurse, was at the market selling the butter she had brought in from the country, Mme. Martin took Theresa to the market and left her with her foster mother; there she remained as good as gold until the market closed at midday.

The mother, gazing at her child with affection, predicted that she would be beautiful, and her prediction turned out to be true. Theresa's looks were not regal, but she had a soft, sweet beauty about her. When Theresa was nine months old, Mme. Martin wrote of her to Pauline, who was a school girl at the Convent of the Visitation: "She seems to me very intelligent. I think she will have a nice disposition; she is always smiling and gives me the impression of being one of the predestined ones!" When eighteen months old she was established queen of the house. She was exceedingly fond of her mother, on whom she lavished caresses. "Not always disinterested ones," Mme. Martin used to say, with a twinkle in her eyes. If Theresa wanted a trifle, a toy of some sort, in order to obtain it she began by affectionately kissing her mother, and she always found this method profitable.

Even with Jesus that was always her way. She was ready first with her love and she seemed to obtain everything. Nothing was denied her, and Jesus worked miracles through her.

Who would have thought that one of her favorite pastimes would be to ride on a swing? Her mother was nervous at first, because the child preferred to stand up on the swing, but the little one was very sure of herself and held on to the rope, never letting go. If she did not consider that the swing was being pushed hard enough, she would soon let the culprit know.

Her entire short life was a flight on high, ever soaring toward perfection. She ever held herself morally erect, holding on to the two ropes of faith and love to save herself from falling—a faith that hopes all from him who can give all; a love that gives all without counting the cost.

St. Augustine used to say, "Love, and do as you please." It was with such a love and complete confidence in God that Theresa spent her whole life, accepting with serenity all that he sent, whether he sent her consolations or whether he left her in darkness and desolation. She would say: "I love him so that I am always contented with whatever he does.... Moreover I redouble my love for him when he hides himself from my faith."

To the great joy of her mother, when Theresa was only twenty-two months old, she first showed signs of love for Jesus. Having been taken to church, she was so interested in the sacred functions that she was always eager to attend them. Every Sunday she insisted on going with the others to Vespers, which she called her "Mass." One Sunday she was taken for a walk instead. She was inconsolable, and began to scream at the top of her voice that she wanted to go to "Mass." Although it had begun to rain, she wriggled out of the arms of the nurse and ran as fast as her little legs would carry her in the direction of the church. She was soon caught and unceremoniously taken home, but she continued to cry for a long time. "Mass" had been missed for that day, at least.

Her good parents, who had been so anxious about her in her infancy, seeing her now healthy and strong, thanked God daily for having spared her. Unfortunately, so many people implore God for favors which they forget all about once they have received them.

M. Martin's gratitude showed itself in his many penances and the pilgrimages he made to various famous shrines, especially those of our Blessed Lady, and his renewed assiduity to the Nocturnal Adoration. Theresa's mother's gratitude was shown by a close union with God and a more diligent study of spiritual perfection.

Mme. Martin's letters to Pauline are enchanting in their simplicity and spontaneity. They are a delicate and loving analysis of the heart of a mother: they are pen pictures and make us "see." For instance:

"Celine and Theresa are inseparable; it would be impossible to find two sisters more united. When Celine is called to her lessons, Theresa is all in tears, 'Oh! dear! what is to become of her! Her best friend is taken from her.' Marie then takes pity on her and lets her accompany her about the house. The poor little soul tries so hard to be good. She will sit quietly on a chair for hours at a time, either threading beads or hemming a duster. She doesn't dare move, and every now and then heaves deep sighs, especially when her needle becomes unthreaded, as it frequently does. She doesn't yet know how to thread it and is afraid to ask Marie for fear of interrupting her at her work. Presently you see two big tears run down her cheeks, but Marie notices and comes to the rescue. She threads the needle, and the dear little angel is all smiles again." And in another letter: "This dear little person is our great consolation. She will grow up good, as I can see the seeds of it already. She talks of nothing but God and would not neglect her prayers for anything in the world. I wish you could hear her reciting her little fables. I have never seen or heard anything so sweet."

Sometimes this happy mother had some different tales to tell of her darling. She was proud of her frankness and the sincerity that made her acknowledge any fault. One day she relates that Theresa inadvertently broke a vase of which she knew her mother was very fond. Immediately she ran to her to make a confession, and her mother could not altogether hide her displeasure at the accident. The poor child went away sobbing, but shortly returned to say, "Don't fret, mother darling. As soon as I begin to earn money I will buy a new vase." She was then three years old. Her mother remarked to Pauline: "You see I shall have to wait some time before I get my vase."

Their love for Theresa, however, was never allowed to degenerate into weakness. At first the father, finding her winning ways irresistible, was a bit inclined to spoil her. For instance, when he came home in the evening, the moment she heard his key in the door she would run to meet him. He would let her sit on his foot and be carried thus into the sitting room, a mode of progression that gave the child great delight. Mme. Martin would smilingly reprove him for always giving into the child's whims. "How can I help it," he would reply, "she is the Queen!"

At times, though, the "queen" could be stubborn. She

was amusing herself on her swing one afternoon when her father called to her, "Come and kiss me, little Queen." Her reply was, "You must come for it, Papa." He refused and walked away. The child understood that though she might be called a "queen," a daddy was the king of the family and as such must always be obeyed. Marie was present and scolded her, saying: "How naughty to answer Papa like that!" Theresa got off the swing immediately, and the whole house resounded with her cries.

In her letters to Pauline, Mme. Martin would occasionally mention some tiny fault: a little obstinacy, or even ambition; mere trifles, but, nevertheless, a comfort to us to read about in our daily conflict with the many temptations of human nature.

Mme. Martin, shortly before her death, wrote in a letter to Mother Agnes of Jesus: "I used to rack my brains to remember every little episode of the child's life to write and tell you about, as I could see how you and all her sisters used to love to hear every little incident, to the exclusion of all other news." Mother Agnes declared that her mother sometimes magnified the little defects of Theresa, just to make a better story.

When Theresa herself was questioned about this she replied simply: "I think you must be right, in a way, because I can remember that even before I was three years old it was never necessary to scold me by means of correction. A single word, like a gentle reproof, was quite enough, and would have been sufficient to make me understand and weep for my defects for the rest of my life."

She added, however: "I was in good hands. Neither Mother nor Marie would ever have allowed nature to conquer grace." They did all in their power to foster every good impulse and to develop all her good qualities of mind and heart.

Her mother never passed over any little roguish trick and always showed her displeasure at any little imperfection. This displeasure was quite sufficient punishment for Theresa who loved her dearly.

To please her mother, Theresa learned very early in life to overcome herself. From that motive she rose to the one of pleasing Jesus, her Love, thus elevating to the supernatural sphere her little victories.

Marie found an efficacious means of multiplying these little victories on the part of Celine and Theresa. She had schooled herself at the convent of the Visitation to count her sacrifices by means of little beads on a string, kept entirely for this purpose. The children became so enthusiastic over this idea that a gentle rivalry sprang up between them; they would vie with each other to see how many sacrifices they could make in a day.

When the mother saw Theresa's little hand go stealthily into her pocket to push up one more bead, she would smile to herself and thank God in her heart.

Playing in the garden under the bushes the two little sisters would count up their triumphs together which they called "practices." The beauty of it was that the combined fingers of their little hands hardly sufficed for these mathematical calculations. One day a neighbor overheard their lively discussion about the "practices" and the number of them, but she could not make out what the children were talking about. She looked over the wall and asked the children to explain. In the simplest way possible, and with no trace of shyness, they explained all to her. The woman went away greatly edified.

Among Theresa's many victories were those over her impulsive nature, such as rising over her anger, and, most marvelous of all in a child, suffering in silence. Yes, for love of Jesus, she concealed her pains and aches; her sacrifices for him were real ones.

One day, for example, she came home red-faced and over-heated, as she had run to the fields and back to gather some flowers. To understand well the full value of this sacrifice one must know that she was, even then, very fond of flowers, as she was all the rest of her life. She loved them for their beauty and simplicity, as they were so much in harmony with the simple beauty of her own soul. It seemed to her that it had taken her hours to weave a garland for her altar out of the flowers she had picked, and just when she was so busy with them, Granny Martin, without in the least realizing the gravity of her offense, asked for the bouquet for her own little altar. Theresa did not hesitate an instant; she gave them to her one by one up to the very last. Only Celine realized her dreadful disappointment, when she saw the big tears rise and cloud her beautiful eyes; tears that were impossible for her to suppress. You will say no doubt, that every properly brought up child will do the same. Certainly, but being obliged to be polite does not remove the bitterness of the sacrifice, and no one will deny that it was a very big one for a child only four years old.

Often in her transports of love Theresa would wish people to die, even her mother and father. Very naturally they reproved her, but her logic was not at fault. Hadn't they always told her that heaven was a place of perfect happiness, and that one had to die to get there? Well, then, what was there that could be strange in her wishing her loved ones to die? She loved them so dearly and she wanted them to be happy.

One time she asked her mother: "Am I a good little girl?" "Yes, dear, you are a good little girl," she responded. Theresa added: "If I weren't good, perhaps I should be sent to hell, but I know what I should do. I would run away and hide myself in your arms and then God couldn't touch me!" She was firmly convinced that once safe in her mother's arms God could do nothing to her.

She was a joy to all, and her frankness was extraordinary. It was charming to see her go to her mother to confess some fault. "Mother, I pushed Celine once and I struck her twice, but I won't do either again."

She would be really unhappy until everyone knew of her fault. Once, by accident, she tore a piece of wallpaper. As soon as her father returned from work she ran to Marie, saying: "Quick, tell him about my tearing the wallpaper," and stood there awaiting her sentence like a criminal.

Just about this time Mme. Martin was stricken with a terminal disease, which slowly accomplished its terrible work of destruction.

The Death of Her Mother

While quite young, Zelie Guerin had knocked herself violently against a piece of furniture. This blow led to a swollen gland in her breast. At first slightly painful, it became more so later on, and finally developed into a fibrous tumor.

The heroic woman bore it without complaining for sixteen years, and without any interruption in her strenuous work or neglect to either her religious duties or her family. However, when the pain became acute and almost unbearable, she could no longer conceal her sufferings. Every remedy was tried, but all to no avail; the malady was too advanced and it was now too late.

There was nothing to hope for but a miracle and for this the poor woman ardently prayed, for the sake of her children. But the divine decrees decided differently.

Mme. Martin's eldest sister, Sister Mary Dosithee of the Visitation Convent, had died a holy death in 1877 of consumption. On one of the last days of her life she said to her superior, "O Mother, I can do nothing now. I can only love, trust, and abandon myself to the divine will. I die thus, passing from earth straight to heaven." Mme. Martin knew this and she hoped to obtain a miracle through the prayers of her saintly sister and the intercession of our

31

Blessed Mother Mary. She enlisted the prayers of all her daughters, especially her little Theresa, as the prayers of the innocent always fly straight to the heart of God. Then she started off to Lourdes with her two eldest daughters.

Four times she was bathed in the pool with no favorable results whatsoever, and she wrote to Pauline: "I should have been so happy to be cured for your sakes, my dear children, but our Lady has said to us, as she did to Bernadette: 'I will make you happy, not in this world but in the next.' Do not expect many consolations down here, dear child, because they are merely illusions. As for me, I know what value to set on all earthly pleasures, and if I had nothing further to look forward to I should indeed be miserable."

On her return, her husband, Celine and Theresa were at the station to greet her. Her husband was sad and downcast. For a week he had hoped to receive a telegram announcing the miracle of his wife's cure; the girls could hardly believe that their prayers had not been granted. Mme. Martin was radiant, and almost deceived them into thinking they were mistaken, but her manner was the outcome of her complete and absolute resignation to the will of God.

Her good spirits put new life into all. That month of July, though, was for her a most terrible ordeal; she suffered in agony and had no respite day or night.

"I have my duty to do," she wrote her sister-in-law. "My time is so very short, and there is so much to be done and I must leave all things in order in case of my death. Therefore, I must make the utmost use of the little strength I have left."

To obtain the grace of final perseverance and to give good example to others up to the very last moment, she dragged herself to the parish church early on the first Friday of August for Mass.

At every step she felt as if she had been stabbed by a sword. The excruciating pain forced her to stop every few yards, but she would not give up. In this state of torture she assisted at Mass. From the sacrifice of Calvary she drew the necessary strength to meet her supreme ordeal.

A pleasant episode cheered her last hours. The summer holidays had just begun and the children planned to give her a happy surprise by decorating her room with flowers and awarding the prizes there for schoolwork well done. The poor children little knew what their mother's sufferings were, for she had concealed them so as not to worry them.

"You should have seen my room all festooned with periwinkles and evergreens," she related to her Aunt Guerin. "Two armchairs were prepared for the prize-givers, Louis and myself. Two little ones, dressed in white, marched away with an air of triumph when they had been presented with prizes and garlands: Marie was very proud of her pupils." Toward midnight, on August 28, 1877, Zelie Martin, an ideal mother only forty-seven years of age, left this world to join her little children who had preceded her to heaven. The day after her death M. Martin took Theresa in his arms and said: "Come and kiss your dear mother for the last time." Without hesitation the little girl put her lips to her mother's cold forehead in obedience to her father's wish.

Sister-Teacher

In her last moments this dying mother, already deprived of the power of speech, fixed her eyes on those of her sister-in-law, Mme. Guerin. It was a long, earnest look that conveyed a fervent prayer, a favor asked from the heart of a mother. The other, a mother herself, understood and promised. She gave her word that she would mother these dear, motherless children.

If any promise should be sacred, how much more binding is one made beside a deathbed—a pledge to care for and protect children who are just losing their own natural protectress. Here was a legacy which, coupled with the anguish of parting, manifested an implicit faith that the trust would be kept faithfully. That suppliant look and that promise made M. Martin then and there decide to leave Alençon for good to go to Lisieux, the home of Mme. Martin, and where M. Guerin conducted a well known pharmacy.

Early in November, his five little daughters went to live with their aunt. Their father followed them to Lisieux as soon as he had wound up his business at Alençon.

"It is a charming little house, bright and cheerful," Marie wrote to her father on November 16 of that same year, describing their new home to him. "It is a pleasant home with a nice garden, where Celine and Theresa can run about and play games. The only part I do not like are the stairs, and the approach to the house which is anything but what it ought to be.

"I think and hope, dear father, that you will be happy and comfortable here. We will try to be very good and to make life sweet for you, so as to compensate you in some little way for the enormous sacrifices you are making for our benefit."

It was indeed an enormous sacrifice for the poor man to have to leave his home at Alençon with all its happy memories and the sad, sad memory of his dear wife's suffering and last moments, the home to which he had taken his young bride and where all the children had been born and where some of them had died. It was a complete break with everything that had gone before and had made up his life until that moment.

Lisieux itself had few attractions of its own. It could not compare in any way with Alençon, which was a larger town and a much more cheerful one in which to live.

Little Theresa was the one who least felt the parting with the old home, as she was too young to attach much importance to any four walls and a roof. Besides, youth loves change.

The very day after her mother's death Celine, no doubt feeling already lost without her authority and tender care, threw herself in the arms of Marie and said, "Well, you will be my mother now," and Marie enfolded her in a warm embrace. Theresa would also have selected Marie as mother by proxy. Had she not always been the loving teacher, the safety valve, a real second mother to her all her young life? But she was afraid Pauline's feelings might be hurt if she were forgotten, so she went up to Pauline and hid her face on her breast saying; "And Pauline will be my mother." We shall see this sister a really privileged soul, in her

work of tutor and guide, roles she was so splendidly fitted for with her great mind, her large, loving heart, and
all her fine perception; in short, her mother's delight. Mme.
Martin wrote to her two years before she died: "You are a
real friend to me, you give me courage in all the trials of
my life.... I thank you for being such a joy to all of us. The
good God will recompense you in this world and in the
next, because even in this world we feel so much happier
when we do our duty generously."

When the mother was nearing her end, seeing Pauline
standing by her bedside, she took the girl's hand and
kissed it; almost as if she were transferring to her the
mantle of motherhood and had a vision of how wonderfully Pauline would fulfill that mission.*

What did the mother see? Was the veil of the future lifted for a moment? That respect and veneration plainly
shown by kissing her hand, that mark of homage on the
part of a mother to her own daughter, is it not eloquent?

In educating her little sister, Pauline chose to follow the
lines already set down by her mother: great love, but never
weakness. Her duty was to inculcate noble, holy thoughts,
and to watch over all human affections.

Theresa, who had learned her ABC's early, thought she
knew enough and returned to her toys, but Pauline was
firm and insisted on daily lessons. Theresa was very proud
of the fact that the first word she learned to read by herself was "heaven."

A recompense for a good day's work and the good
marks earned was a walk with her father in the afternoon.
But if the marks were bad the walk had to be foregone; the
lesson mistress was inflexible in this. It is hard to say who

---

* Pauline was like a mother to Theresa after their mother's death, and then, as
prioress at Lisieux, mother to the other two sisters as well. Pope Pius XI, in a
brief, confirmed her as prioress of the Carmelite convent at Lisieux in perpe-
tuum.

suffered more, the father or the child, but M. Martin always upheld Pauline's authority. Pauline was firm with Theresa in everything, at the same time showing love and kindness to her little sister.

Theresa was very timid and nervous, and Pauline, wishing to cure her of this, would send her on errands in the dark to get something from an unlighted room and would take no excuses about it. She reaped the reward of her firmness, for Theresa became quite brave and gradually lost her fears.

Theresa had a generous heart and always had a great thirst for the salvation of souls. Coming in one day tired and hot from running a good deal in the sun, she exclaimed: "O Pauline, if you only knew how thirsty I am!" Pauline thought this a good opportunity to test her virtue, so she asked her: "And would you give up a drink to save a poor sinner?" "Yes, Pauline." But Pauline's tender heart melted at once. She went and drew a glass of fresh water and said: "Drink. You made the sacrifice and that counts." Theresa didn't like to take her at her word, but Pauline explained to her that the moment she said "yes" she consented to the sacrifice, and that now she was to drink under obedience, which was another virtue and would also serve to help a poor sinner.

With her charity for souls she coupled charity for the poor and needy. Monday was the regular day when the poor came and rang the bell at the Martin home; Theresa, who didn't go to school yet like Leonie and Celine, was entrusted with the joy of giving them alms. She would hand it to them with such tender pity in her eyes that this alone would have been a comfort to them. "May God reward you, little Miss," they would smilingly say to her. Then she would scamper off to relate what they had said to Pauline.

Many and many a time she had recourse to her father's wallet when on their walks together she happened to notice a poor person.

She remembered how on the day of her first Holy Communion she saw the face of one who looked sad, and she was much impressed; it was the first time she had come across the "other side of the medal." Her world up to then had contained nothing but beautiful things.

Pauline, who had had charge of her upbringing, had instilled this tender pity for the poor in her heart, and Theresa responded to it conscientiously, as she did to all of Pauline's counsels. To the same saintly and beloved guide she owed her great love of all religious feasts, and she listened absorbedly to the history of them and their mysteries. Perhaps the one dearest to her heart was "Corpus Christi," which yearly brought to her the incomparable joy of strewing flowers before the Blessed Sacrament in the procession. She considered each flower a kiss to the hidden God in the monstrance.

To Pauline, also, she owed the great reverence she always held for priests. This reverence really began at the time of her first Holy Communion, which she made when she was twelve years old.

Ah! If she was not yet to be allowed to receive the divine Body of Jesus, let her at least be near him and see him in every one of his priests. Pauline had warned her: "Theresa, darling, it is not to a man but to God himself that you are going to tell your sins." Theresa was so convinced of this, that she asked Pauline if she ought to tell her confessor that she loved him with her whole heart! Since the priest was no longer himself but transformed into Christ, why shouldn't she make him this loving declaration which she was in the habit of making to our Lord himself?

Pauline taught clearness of thought and simplicity of speech and deportment. What sweet logic the elder sister would use to explain some truth to her childish mind and make her understand an abstract idea. Once Theresa was perturbed to know how people could all be equally happy in heaven, some having a higher degree of glory than others. Clever Pauline had a practical example to convince her, which made her understand what seemed to her a mystery.

She sent Theresa to fetch her father's large tumbler and to bring with her her own little sewing thimble. Then she told her to fill them both to the brim with water. When she had done this, Pauline asked her: "Which of these in your estimation is fullest?" Perplexed, Theresa replied: "But both are as full as can be. Not a drop could be added to either of them without their overflowing."

"Well, and so it shall be with the elect," said Pauline. "No one in heaven can envy anyone else, because each one will have received happiness to the fullest capacity and no one could contain more."

Another time the two sisters were by the sea, sitting on the beach looking at a wonderful sunset. The enormous disc of the sun, shining in all its crimson glory, was slowly and gradually disappearing in the ocean beyond the horizon, leaving a trail of light glistening on the water.

"It is the emblem of the grace that illumines the path of faithful souls," explained Pauline. And Theresa imagined herself as a little boat riding the waters in the path of that light, promising herself never to wander from her Jesus. All Pauline's teachings certainly fell on fruitful soil.

Theresa visibly grew in goodness. That look of predestination which her mother had noticed in the baby's eyes grew more intense, so nearly all could see it. People would turn to look at her in the street and remark to each other: "She scarcely looks as if she were of this earth." A person who had often seen her in church and noticed her rapt look when gazing at the Blessed Sacrament, said: "I wouldn't be surprised if that child died young. But if she doesn't, mark my words, she will be a saint!" There were some who would ask for a lock of her golden hair to keep as a relic. The child might easily have had her head turned with adulation, but from the very first Pauline had profoundly convinced her that nothing in life is of any real importance except God. This child, so holy and mystical, was still quite a child, enjoying the simple pleasures that she shared with her family. She used to count the days until Thursday, which was a half holiday, when she could play with Celine. But even in doing so much good, she always had need of encouragement. If Pauline had not assured her each evening that Jesus loved her and would receive her in paradise, she would have cried all night.

The Father

If Pauline was Theresa's able instructress, her father was her most able supporter.

These two spent many hours in the belvedere terrace at the top of the house, and M. Martin would often pray and meditate there.

Feeling herself nearer heaven at that height, Theresa would join him the moment her lessons were over. What a pair they were: he, with his venerable white head and she, fresh as a rose, with her golden curls that would have delighted any artist's soul. They seemed to attract the eyes of all passers-by. Both the old man and the young child had the same expression, a look that was of heaven and not of earth.

Theresa was always his companion when he went to church and she learned from him how the saints pray. It was with him that she first entered the little church of Carmel, and was told about the holy women hidden behind the veil and the grill, who dedicate themselves to continuous prayer and offer up their sacrifices and immolations for sinners.

She accompanied him when he went to hear sermons, but kept her eyes more constantly fixed on her father's face than on the preacher's, feeling, no doubt, that the very sweetness of her father's expression moved her more than the words of the sermon.

She was also his companion when he went fishing, but her patience was not equal to his. After a very little while she used to retire to the shade of a tree and there sit on the grass and meditate.

Both father and daughter understood the language of nature, a language that elevates the soul more than any other and teaches one to praise one's Maker, and to thank him for the gift of creation and its beauty. While the father patiently awaited a bite from the wary fish, his gaze would rove over the landscape spread before his eyes and he, too, would be lost in wonderment and thanksgiving for all the sweetness and beauty he beheld.

His ear was attuned to the thousand and one sounds that one encounters in the open: the distant note of birds and the feeble noise of myriads of insects, which became more and more perceptible as the quiet of the day increased and which added to all the enchantment and mystery.

With the rustling of the trees, the warbling of the birds, and the humming of the bees, the sound of distant bells mingled with the strains of the town band would come to them borne by the breeze.

The fascination of nature always enraptured Theresa. How eloquent to her was a starry night! Holding fast to her father's hand she would keep her eyes fixed on the heavenly vault. One day she said she found her name written there in stars. In the belt of the constellation Orion she saw a capital T, and was delighted. Much as she loved and admired the starry heavens in all their glory on a clear, calm summer's night, she sensed something far more beautiful beyond them, something she lacked the power to express. Not only did she learn much from her father's example (he was always teaching her new and beautiful things), but to him she owed the greatness of her faith, as well as the profound detachment she felt from the things of this world.

"People," M. Martin would say, "give themselves an infinity of troubles to preserve their life when on the eve of death. They couldn't be more solicitous about it if they still had several centuries to live.

"They behave in like manner toward all the things of this world, scarcely ever giving a thought to the important ones of the next, forgetting that in the hereafter they will be immortal!

"God laughs at their foolishness, for does he not know the exact hour and the moment when they will have to relinquish everything and go to meet him, their Judge?

"This divine decree does not excuse us from taking ordinary care of our health, which is in reality a duty, but to put the cares of the body before those of the soul is wrong. Let us do our best and leave the rest to providence."

The Abbot of Rancé was right: "In vain the sea roars and the waves toss and rage and the ship seems in peril from all the elements. If divine Providence wills it, there will be no shipwreck and nothing will prevent the ship from reaching harbor."

"O father mine," Theresa would exclaim in her enthusiasm, "if the French could hear you, they would make you their King, and I should not be pleased, for you would no longer be mine alone."

In the winter evenings at Les Buissonnets they would all gather round the fire and Theresa would take her place sitting on her father's knee. Marie and Pauline would read aloud for some time out of a paper called *The Liturgical Year*, after which their father, who had a splendid voice, would sing to them. Then they would all go upstairs for night prayers, and there, again, the youngest daughter had the privileged place next to Papa. When the prayers were finished, Pauline would put Theresa to bed. Then came the inevitable questions: "Have I been good today, Pauline? Is Jesus pleased with me? Will the angels fly all round my bed?" Pauline's reply was always in the affirmative.

Prophetic Vision

M. Martin had to absent himself often from Les Buissonnets on private affairs. During one of these absences an extraordinary thing happened.

On a summer afternoon between two and three o'clock, Theresa, then seven years old, was looking out of the window into the garden. In her soul, as in all nature that day, all was light, quiet, and repose. Her sisters were at work in the next room. She was alone. Suddenly her sisters heard her call out, "Papa, Papa!" She seemed as if she were in anguish, her voice was trembling with terror.... They ran to her. Marie reached her first and said, "Why are you calling Papa when he is in Alençon?"

Theresa, with visible emotion, tried to explain as best she could what she had seen. It was a man, exactly like her father, advancing towards her in the garden. He was of her father's height and build, but bent nearly double and he seemed old. She could not see his face, because it was covered by a black veil.

She had called to him. He didn't answer but passed on as if he hadn't heard, and then, when he reached a clump of pine trees at the end of the garden, he disappeared.

The sisters tried to persuade Theresa that it might have been the nurse playing a prank, but the nurse denied doing any such thing. They asked her whether she had seen anyone in the garden and she denied this also. A complete search of house and garden revealed not even a trace of an intruder. Still the child insisted that she had seen a man and that he was exactly her father's height and build, only bent and old.

They told her to put it from her mind and think no more about it. They questioned each other afterwards wondering with anguish what could be the meaning of such a strange happening.

Not to think of it anymore! It was easy to say, but the poor child found it beyond her power to do so. She could see the mysterious and terrible vision before her eyes all the time. If she had only been able to lift the thick veil that disguised the features, she would then have understood the mystery! In the depths of her soul, however, she felt that some day it would be revealed to her. That day did dawn, years later.

We will anticipate and recount some of the events that led up to this prophetic vision of Theresa's childhood.

In 1885, M. Martin, urged by a priest then living in Lisieux, undertook an extensive missionary journey into Germany, Austria, Greece and Italy. The many beautiful churches, as well as the gorgeous scenery in these countries, were a feast to the eyes of one who had traveled little and had never dreamed of seeing so many wonderful things.

He wrote enthusiastically of the sights to Marie—his "diamond"; his "good Leonie"; the "intrepid" Celine; and the "Queen of his heart," not forgetting the "priceless pearl of Carmel," Pauline (with these affectionate titles he dubbed his daughters). His deepest emotions were stirred in Rome, where his Catholic soul thrilled with joy. He begged Marie to tell Pauline: "Tell my pearl that I am too happy; this state cannot last!" Was this an omen?

Upon his arrival in Milan on his return journey, he felt that everything on earth was vanity and affliction of spirit. He realized the transient quality of earthly things and at the end of this journey he was left with a greater longing than ever for his eternal home.

Here in a few words he gives us an insight into his heart:

"All I see is beautiful, splendid, but it is nevertheless only a terrestrial beauty and nothing can really satisfy our hearts except the Beatific Vision. Soon I shall have the great joy of being among you again. This is a joy that approaches nearer than any other to that heavenly one."

The happiness he had experienced in Rome he managed to recapture three years later in the Church of Notre Dame at Alençon. It was the reward of God to a father, good and just, generously offering his Isaac in the person of his little Theresa who had just entered Carmel. He preferred a love that gives to one that receives, and if at Rome he felt almost too happy and foresaw sorrow coming to him, now at Alençon he asked for it; he offered himself on Calvary.

"My daughters," he said, the first day he went to Carmel and talked to his daughters collectively. "My daughters, the many graces and consolations that I have received in the Church of Notre Dame d'Alençon have been such that I made the following prayer: 'My God, I am too happy, it is too much! Yes, I am too happy. It isn't possible to go to paradise thus. I wish to suffer something for your sake' and I offered myself...." The word victim died on his lips. He scarcely dared to pronounce it before his daughters, but he knew the offering had been accepted. About two years before this he had been struck down with paralysis, from which he had been completely cured.

After offering himself as a victim in union with the Divine One on Calvary, he had a second and a third stroke which at first took away the partial use of his legs and, finally, completely paralyzed them, depriving him at the same time of all his intellectual faculties.

"What a terrible trial this loss of reason, for a father of a family!" exclaimed Father Petitot, the Dominican. "It is the extinguishing of the sun, the world of thought and everything that is of the spirit; to fall into darkness and chaos!"

The bent old man seen by Theresa in her inexplicable vision comes at once to our thoughts. It is indeed her afflicted father struck with paralysis who, with feeble steps, is approaching the tomb.

We may ask ourselves, "Why was this very sad vision granted to a child barely seven years old?" Theresa herself says that God in his infinite wisdom and mercy wished to soften this terrible blow in proportion to her tender years by preparing her for it.

Father Petitot admits this, but also adds another reason. From the passion and suffering of her father, Theresa will be better able to understand the Passion of Christ. The veiled features of her father will give her an insight into the mysteries of humiliations concealed in the adorable face of our suffering Lord who became the opprobrium of men and an object of pity to the people.

The same author draws for us a wonderful similarity between two visions: that of Isaiah about the Savior and that of the little child about her father. These are his words:

"This prophetic vision about the father, a father so good, so full of piety, generous and blameless, is that of the just man offered as a victim for the sins of his brethren, the sinners of the world.

"Now, this vision recalls to us by a necessary coordination of ideas that of Isaiah the prophet. Theresa looked upon that as the foundation of her belief.

"The man seen by Isaiah in this most extraordinary of prophecies is a victim offered in holocaust, weighed down with the burden of the sins of others: 'He offered himself because he willed it, and God put upon him all our iniquities.'

"Interrogated, he did not answer: 'non aperuit os suum.' His countenance is hidden and veiled, 'absconditus vultus ejus.' Similarly the man seen by Theresa is a voluntary victim; he does not reply at the sound of her voice; his countenance is veiled.

"Thus the prophetic vision of the father, and of the just man suffering for others seen by Isaiah, correspond. Without doubt this resemblance, these symbolic similarities so impressed on the mind of Theresa, will help her to penetrate, providentially, the real character of the Messiah and the ineffable mysteries hidden in the divine features of the Savior of the world.

"As the adorable features of our Redeemer were veiled during the Passion, so were those of his faithful servant, Theresa's father, during the long days of his humiliation, so as to shine with greater splendor in the day of glory in heaven."

Let us note what one of her fellow religious at Carmel said about the saint:

"It was while at Carmel and when she was enduring this terrible trial in connection with her father that Sister Theresa attached herself more and more closely to the mysteries of the Passion. It was then that she obtained permission to add to her name in religion the words 'and of the Holy Face,' and I believe that after her death it was this that inspired Sister Genevieve (Celine) to paint her masterpiece of the Holy Face taken from the Holy Shroud of Turin."

We do not doubt the vision of the child Theresa, since it came true to the letter. In the initial stages of his malady M. Martin covered his head with a black cloth, just as Theresa had seen in her vision. This prophetic vision was ordained by divine Providence to give her a better understanding of the character of the suffering Redeemer.

Heavy trials are necessary for the penetrating of certain supernatural truths. When such trials are preceded by a prophetic vision, how much more does the privileged soul have to apply herself to meditation in an endeavor to probe the deep meaning of them!

Sister Theresa had a special love for the Holy Face, as portrayed in the Sixth Station of the Cross, when Christ imprinted his sacred features on Veronica's veil. At seven years of age Theresa had a prophetic vision of the Holy Face. Although so young, she clearly understood that sanctity consists, essentially, in imitation of Christ in a hidden, suffering life.

What was a scandal to the Jews and folly for the Greeks who would not accept it (that is, Christ Crucified as a symbol of the life of a Christian), Theresa accepted and made her goal from childhood. We shall see later how our beloved little saint showed her heroism during her long trial. We will content ourselves by adding that the final triumph of that aged father, so dear to God and to his neighbor, came on the day of the "clothing" of his "little Queen." Heaven and earth combined to make her happy; nothing was lacking, not even the snow she wished for, which fell so unexpectedly that very day.

Attired in a magnificent gown of white velvet, trimmed with beautiful Alençon lace and bordered with swans' down, Theresa, radiant with joy, seemed, in all truth, a queen. When she kissed her father good-bye she little knew the Calvary that was awaiting him, nor, for that matter, the Calvary that would come to her so soon.

Once before his death M. Martin was brought to Carmel to see his daughter, to take his last farewell of her. Oh, what a sad visit for both of them! However, our Lord permitted for their mutual comfort at parting, a ray of light to illuminate his mind.

It was on July 29, 1894, that M. Martin went to receive the crown of martyrs, after giving a last and loving look at Celine, who had been his dear nurse.

The School Girl

After this lengthy digression we will return to the childhood of St. Theresa.

In 1881 everything was changed in her young life. In the autumn of that year Theresa went daily as an extern student to the Benedictine Convent at Lisieux with Celine and her cousin Marie Guerin.

Celine had been a pupil there for some time but all was new to little Theresa. The former was vivacious, friendly and happy; the latter shy, timid, and sensitive to excess, full of feeling, with a deep sentiment that very rarely shows itself outwardly.

Theresa had seldom before left home. When she did, it was to visit some other very happy home like that of her cousins, the Guerins. She had no contact with anyone who was not of gentle birth, affectionate, and of refined manners. Vulgar, rude speech, and gross manners astonished and repelled her, as she was utterly unacquainted with them. This tender flower, transported into an open field, noisy and rough as a school of about sixty girls of all ages can be, felt completely out of her element, and she suffered a good deal.

She was only eight and a half when she entered, and was immediately placed in a class with girls far older than herself. One of them, a girl of fourteen of limited intelligence, became very jealous of Theresa when she found that she was usually first in composition and a favorite with the nuns. Theresa had to suffer petty persecution from this girl. She was too timid and gentle to be able to defend herself and her spirit of abnegation prompted her to bear all things in silence. Her only solace was tears shed in secrecy, known only to the heart of Jesus.

The happiest time of the day for her was returning home to her family each evening. With what joy would she perch on her father's knee and report to him the marks she had received for her composition and conduct. He invariably rewarded her once a week with a bright silver piece of money, which she would treasure in her purse to give to the poor.

From 1877 to 1886 Theresa went through a period of darkness. Over those gifts that God had showered upon her had been drawn a veil. These are Celine's words: "She was passing through the world unobserved. One great cause of her silence was an extreme timidity that kept her monosyllabic and almost tongue-tied. She was at times paralyzed with fear. There were occasions when she exposed herself to adverse criticisms through her very silence. She suffered a great deal just then with severe headaches, but the main source of her sufferings was her terrible sensitivity to everything.

"It is very important to notice though, that in spite of this weakness, she was in those years really a strong character and I deduce this strength from the fact that, in spite of all she felt, she never once neglected one of her duties. I never observed in her an exclamation of annoyance, a hasty word, or the minimum lack of virtue. Her mortifications were incessant, and in every one of her actions. She seemed never to lose an opportunity to offer some sacrifice to God.

"In these trials of her adolescence I could see the finger of God, training her in humility. She herself said: 'I had much need of that austere training, inasmuch as I would not have been insensible to praise.'"

This terrible sensitivity of Theresa caused her to cry for the least thing, and when she had been consoled she would cry for having given way to tears. She recognized this great weakness in herself and speaks of her "conversion," or the change which came over her at Christmas, 1886. This is how the change occurred:

Theresa and her father, with Celine and Leonie, were returning home from the midnight Mass, all in a state of excitement at the idea of finding well-filled stockings hanging up for each of them on the drawing-room fireplace. She was a big girl now, it is true, but she remained the baby of the family.

The father had always been the first to share in her joy and her happy exclamations on discovering each fresh surprise. But this time, quite contrary to custom, he seemed displeased about it. Even this attitude of his was no doubt ordained by Providence.

Going up to her room to remove her outdoor things, Theresa heard her father say in resolute tones to her sisters: "Let it be the last time, then. It is too childish for a big girl like Theresa." Was it possible that it was her dear, lenient, and kind-hearted daddy talking like that?

It was the first time she had ever heard that tone from him and she found it difficult to restrain her tears. Dear Celine, whom those words had hurt even more than Theresa, flew up the stairs to her and whispered in her ear: "Don't come down for a few minutes, dear. Just wait to compose yourself. You might cry too much over your treasures if you went now."

But it wasn't so. The child, gathering all her strength, removed every trace of a tear and went quietly and calmly down the stairs to her father who had seemingly forgotten his slight outburst and was already handing her the "surprises." Theresa received them with a joy and spontaneity that Celine marveled at. What could have happened? Jesus, to whom she had frantically appealed for help, had restored her calm and given her courage, thus enabling her to gain a victory over self. One's first victory is often the first link in a long chain of uninterrupted acts of virtue which gradually lead a person to self-mastery.

Before she attained this mastery, however, she had to school herself for years. She had entered the convent school in 1881 and this triumph of grace happened in 1886. Five years of self-denial! And she was only a child.

Her usual expression was sweet and smiling, and her manners were gentle and amiable. She had a tender piety. An implicit obedience was hers to the least command. She avoided noisy games as she did school intrigues. Such was her school life, which would have been happier but for her terrible sensitiveness. It was mainly due to this defect of hers that the good nuns did not fully appreciate the treasure that had been confided to their care.

For instance, Theresa had need of silent prayer, that prayer which rises to God from the heart without any need of words. It rises to the beloved on the wings of meditation and contemplation. Formulas confused her. The book of prayers on which she was obliged to keep her eyes fixed only worried and hampered her, and so she would fix her eyes on the Tabernacle or, at other times, would close them to better concentrate on him who dwelt ever in her heart, but at once she was recalled to her duty.

"Theresa, always inclined to meditate, was great of soul and much given to thought," said Pauline. "I found her far too serious and too advanced for her age."

Play, noise, games and petty squabbles—none of these were for her. She missed the pleasures of a garden, such as she had been accustomed to all her life. At the Abbey there was only a severe rectangular courtyard and, therefore, her one joy in the day was to return home in the evening.

As the nuns did not allow the girls to stand about talking during recreation, Theresa did her best to conform to the rules and played with the others. No one knew what she endured during those times, doing things contrary to her ideal in life.

These contacts with those of less refined natures and diverse characters, whose outlook on life did not provide them with the spiritual delicacy of Theresa, furnished Theresa with innumerable opportunities for a silent martyrdom of five years duration. Throughout this trial she blessed and thanked God for his continual flow of graces.

She tried to make friends with one of the sisters, who was an object of affection for so many of the girls, but Theresa's intense shyness prevented her making any headway. She made two friends among the girls, but these friendships did not deepen.

To this accumulation of small things which comprised her martyrdom as a child, she had a secret and greater one, that of scruples. Only those who have endured them can speak knowingly of the torture they can be to a sensitive mind.

She had a most terrible blow just at this time, too. Pauline, her beloved adopted mother, who held in her dear hands Theresa's heart and soul, had just announced her intention of entering Carmel. The thought of this fresh separation, so soon after the loss of her dear mother, was almost too much for Theresa to bear. Her grief was renewed each time she visited Carmel because, on account of her youth, she was permitted to spend only a few minutes with Pauline. During these few minutes she found it difficult at times to utter a word, choked as she was with tears. So much tension, such silent and profound grief in one so young, ended by undermining her health.

The devil, envious of Theresa's further conquests, seemed to wish to crush her will. He endeavored with all his might to agitate her and make her lose the mastery of her soul, but God looks after those who confide implicitly in him.

Next to Pauline in her affections was Celine, the sister nearer to her in age and her playmate from her earliest youth. She was also very fond of her little cousin, Marie Guerin, who, as she says in her autobiography, "used to let me choose my own games."

They were very fond of pretending to be anchorites. They had heard of the hermits of the desert and made up their minds to try to imitate them to the best of their ability. Each had a little hut, a plot of grass, and a bed of fertilized soil where they cultivated what they considered a garden. They were much given to contemplation, but since they had various other duties, they had to take turns at the contemplative life. All this was performed with laudable and serious attention and often they continued the game of pretense even in the streets. The two hermits walked along reciting the Rosary, using their fingers for beads so as not to attract too much attention. One day the anchorite, Theresa, forgot she was not in the desert, and before eating a large bun saved from breakfast she stopped and solemnly made a large sign of the cross over it, much to the amusement of the passers-by.

Theresa and Marie wished also to imitate the anchorites in modesty of the eyes. Holding hands as they walked along, one would shut her eyes and let herself be guided by the other. Trouble occurred, however, when both decided to close their eyes at the same time. They were on the sidewalk and considered themselves quite safe. A grocer on their route had piled up some cases of merchandise outside the door of his shop, and our would-be hermits marched straight into them scattering the goods all over the sidewalk and into the gutter, and causing a fearful commotion. The proprietor rushed out shaking his fist and shouting what he was going to do to the culprits, who by this time were some distance away for, with a singular loss of dignity, they had taken to their heels and fled!

On August 15, 1895, Marie Guerin entered the Carmelite Convent and took for her name in religion Sister Marie of the Holy Eucharist. She was remarkable for her great spirit of poverty and her patience during a long illness and much pain. One day she said: "I do not know if I have suffered well, but I almost feel as if Theresa communicates her feelings to me and I emulate them. Oh! if I could only die like her of love. It wouldn't be so surprising after all because I, too, belong to that little band called the 'legion of little souls' that she asked God for. I wish to die telling Jesus how much I love him." This desire of hers was realized. She died on April 14, 1905, at the age of thirty-four, and her very last words were: "I am not afraid to die. O what peace! One must never dread suffering. He always gives strength for it. My Jesus, I love you."

A Smile from Mary
in the Hour of Anguish and Trial

M. Martin was in Paris with Marie and Leonie when a telegram urgently recalled him to Lisieux.

His little Theresa was ill and the doctors, unable to diagnose the malady, acknowledged that they were unable to give any relief. Later on she regained her health, but at that time one could only say she was as delicate as a lily.

M. Guerin had no real idea of the depth of the sensitiveness of his young niece's character or of her precocious intelligence and during one whole evening, in the absence of her father, he talked to Theresa of her mother. She cried much, and then spoke at great length, opening her heart to him, revealing thoughts and sentiments he had not suspected. What a revelation to the uncle who had constituted himself her tutor! He came to the conclusion that she was too advanced and needed distractions suitable to her age.

He realized now that her silence and reserve were occasioned by deep and serious thoughts.

He had been planning for future holidays, when Theresa fell seriously ill.

It was only on the day that her sister Pauline received

the habit that she showed any marked improvement. Therefore, Theresa was taken that day to Carmel and had the ineffable joy of sitting on her "little mother's" lap and receiving her caresses, as of old. On her return home Theresa suffered a relapse.

Confronted with the utter impotence of human remedies, M. Martin, in great faith and hope, wrote to the Church of Our Lady of Victories in Paris, begging for a novena of Masses for the life and health of his beloved daughter.

So many earnest prayers for her cure would surely touch the heart of our heavenly Mother, to whom Theresa was as dear as she was to Jesus himself. When Theresa saw her father give several gold pieces to Marie and tell her to send them to our Lady of Victories for Masses, his look of deep sorrow cut his little queen to the heart. She told them afterwards she longed above all things to have been able to spring out of bed, and say: "I am cured," but the moment had not yet arrived. All hoped for a miracle.

On the following Sunday, during the novena, Marie left her with Leonie for a while and went into the garden. A few minutes later Theresa softly called: "Marie, Marie." Leonie was accustomed to this frequent summons and did not heed. Theresa called louder: "Marie," and when the latter came running in, the invalid did not seem to recognize her and continued to call. Marie was perturbed. She whispered something to Leonie and left the room.

Presently Theresa, whom Leonie had by now seated in a chair by the window, saw Marie coming across the garden with arms extended, calling softly to her: "Theresa, my little Theresa, here I am," but this ruse was no more successful than the former, and Marie, almost in despair, flung herself on her knees near the foot of Theresa's bed. Turning towards the statue of our Blessed Lady she implored help as a mother would for her child. Leonie and Celine followed her example, and the three of them uttered such a cry of faith that it forced the Gate of Heaven.

The little patient not having found any relief or help so far, also turned her head in the direction of the statue and prayed fervently that the gentle Queen of Heaven might take pity on her in her sufferings.

Immediately it seemed as if the statue had come to life. The Blessed Virgin looked so beautiful that they were unable to describe the supernatural beauty of her features. What touched them most was the heavenly sweetness of her smile.

Down little Theresa's cheeks coursed two big tears; then she smiled also.... She was cured!

Our Blessed Lady had smiled at her and she felt no more terrors and no more pain. She recognized her nurse, who questioned her with her eyes to see if it was really true. Were the terrible days and nights of anguish over and was the return to health complete?

Marie's questioning eyes seemed, however, to ask her further, to try as it were to probe the innermost secrets of her heart. Theresa, wondering at her changed attitude, confessed that although she was completely cured of her recent illness a certain bitterness of spirit remained. This sorrow overshadowed her for four years. She was finally relieved of it at the foot of the statue of Our Lady of Victories in the church of that name in Paris.

The first thing she did was to go speedily to Carmel and inform Pauline of the miracle of her cure. Pauline, having made her profession, was now Sister Agnes of Jesus. On this great occasion the whole Community came to the parlor, and with rapt attention listened to the account of Theresa's cure. Unfortunately, to the embarrassment of little Theresa, some facts had been exaggerated, for which she feared that she might have been responsible. A few words of explanation sufficed to clarify the matter.

The First Kiss from Jesus

Our Lady's smile was like a preparation for the first kiss from Jesus. Between the two, however, it seems that there was a moment when the world did, after all, have some attraction for Theresa. For a short while she wavered toward beauty, praise, and human affection.

After the miracle, Theresa remained for a time somewhat delicate, and her father deemed it wise to send her to the country to recuperate. He accepted for her two invitations extended by old friends of the family who lived in beautiful old villas with every comfort and luxury, leading a worldly life of pleasure and ease.

Theresa found herself admired and sought after and thoroughly spoiled. Looking around she considered the world, indeed, a desirable place, but this was only a passing thought and a very natural one for a person who had never been exposed to such temptation before. Then her soul recoiled from such thoughts. She realized that she could never really belong to anyone but Jesus and that she must therefore give up pleasures of the world if she wished to have real, lasting happiness with him.

The effect of this experience was to remain with her throughout life. She now saw clearly the perils of the world of pleasure, and felt sorry for those poor souls who, like moths in a destructive flame, lose the great gift of immortality by running after temporary earthly joys.

All this happened in 1883. The following year she was to make her First Holy Communion. In the first meeting of hers with Jesus, she was to bind herself forever to him with indissoluble bonds.

How she had yearned for years for that happy day! In those days children were not allowed to approach the Sacred Banquet until the age of eleven. The diocese of Lisieux and Bayeux was particularly strict in this respect. The age limit counted from January 1, and, because Theresa was born on January 2, she had to wait another year, much to her great sorrow.

Frequently she implored her sisters to take her with them to the Eucharistic feast, even when she was quite little. She loved Jesus, she said, and did not see why she should be kept from receiving him in Holy Communion.

She said to them: "I will squeeze myself quite close to the altar. I am so little no one notices me, so perhaps I shall be able to receive my Jesus!"

She was dreadfully disappointed at having to wait this extra year, and one day, as she caught sight of Msgr. Hugonin, Bishop of Bayeux and Lisieux, hurrying to the station with his Vicar General, she implored Marie: "Oh, do let me run after him and ask his permission to let me make my First Communion this year!" Marie had to restrain her by force.

Her preparation was a long and arduous one, though sweet to her because of her great thirst for the Sacrament and her attraction to religious instructions. Every evening, in the study or in the garden, the two sisters, the eldest and the youngest, would meet and talk about the great event.

Marie put forth all her spiritual energies trying to make her little sister understand this ineffable "gift of God." While Marie taught her by word of mouth, Sister Agnes of Jesus did not forget she was her "little mother" and assisted her with her saintly prayers. She gave Theresa a book written by herself on the value of the little garland of the Blessed Virgin Mary. This booklet showed a flower on every page with the words: "I have gathered some" followed by a pious invocation or an act of love, as mystical perfume of the flower gathered by her. Every evening the child was to record the numbers of her "flowers" for that day, and in three months she found to her joy that she had made 2,773 acts of love and 818 sacrifices.

Marie would not give in to Theresa's desire to spend half an hour, or even a quarter of an hour, every night in a "heart to heart" talk with Jesus. Marie thought that Theresa was already advanced in her understanding of spiritual things and thought she had better exercise a certain amount of restraint. The sweet child gave in at once with her usual graciousness. Without in the least thinking she was giving herself up to real mental prayer she would go and hide herself in the curtains of the four-poster bed, so as to be entirely hidden. When questioned as to what she did there, she admitted she thought of God, of the shortness of life, and of eternity.

Marie, with her great and generous love, imparted to Theresa knowledge of all the beautiful things of life. At the same time, as the warriors of old brought up their children with the knowledge of weapons and their use, Marie instructed Theresa concerning the combat of life, exciting love as she showed her the glorious palm of martyrdom. She described eternal riches, which are easy to accumulate each day, and the folly of neglecting to amass them when one could easily do so by exerting a little effort.

She was so eloquent that Theresa listened spellbound and thought her sister could, indeed, conquer all hearts should she choose to do so, that no sinner however hardened could resist her, and that they would, in fact, at once

leave their perishable joys and henceforth strive only after the things of heaven. The three months' training passed
very quickly. She would soon enter school and go into
retreat with the other girls. How she loved silence! As there
were not many girls preparing for their First Holy Communion, the good Sisters could give more individual attention to each of them. These were days of quiet joy for
Theresa and all through life she recalled them.

At last the great day dawned! Theresa and the other
girls, dressed in white with white veils and wreaths of
white roses, walked devoutly to the chapel by twos for the
Mass during which they would receive Jesus in Holy Communion. With inexpressible joy Theresa gave herself entirely to him!

She shed tears of happiness.

"Why does she cry?" whispered her companion. Perhaps she has some scruple of conscience.... Perhaps she
misses her mother and her sister who is a Carmelite. No,
Theresa could have told them it was none of these things.
It was simply because, when the whole joy of heaven en-
ters one poor little heart, that heart, weak, mortal and ex-
iled, gets too full and tears flow. By a marvelous coinci-
dence the day that Theresa for the first time united herself
to Jesus as a victim of love, Pauline, by means of her religious profession was offering herself as a victim of love
to that same Jesus. In the afternoon Theresa went to Carmel, and she and her sister had many wonderful and beautiful things to talk about.

Before going to bed that night Theresa wrote down a
few simple resolutions:

1. I will never let myself be discouraged.
2. I will recite the "Memorare" every day.
3. I will seek to humiliate my pride.

She was, indeed, always simple and direct in all she did;
and there was no guile in her nature.

The next day she began thirsting again to receive the Holy Eucharist. Formerly she longed for Jesus because she had never received him. Now more than ever did she long for the One of whose sweetness she had so recently tasted.

Unfortunately the rule was that children could receive Holy Communion only on feast days. Marie, who had instructed her all through this important time, did not consider her task done, but the evening before each subsequent Communion she gave her further instructions and spiritual conferences in order to incite her love and her piety.

One evening she took for her subject "Suffering," its advantages, and its part in our human existence; adding, however, that perhaps it might not be God's will for her.

On the contrary, Theresa remembered that at her First Communion she had experienced a burning desire to bear her share of the Cross and she realized with certainty at the time, that her wish would be granted.

She felt a great joy at the thought of being able to share in our dear Savior's sufferings, but to undertake them would require strength, and this she requested with all the powers of her soul. She asked the Holy Spirit, the Divine Paraclete, always to come to her assistance and bring his gifts.

Veni, Sancte Spiritus

"Theresa received the Sacrament of Confirmation on June 4, 1884," wrote Celine, "and the few days preceding it are firmly impressed on my memory.

"She, usually so calm and collected, was not in the least her usual self, and looking at her you could see she was thrilling with some inner excitement and enthusiasm. I expressed my surprise at seeing her in such an exalted mood. She explained to me that what she understood of the grace of this Sacrament was that the Holy Spirit in coming into her soul would take entire possession of it forevermore.

"There was such ardor in her bearing, such fire in her speech that I, myself, felt supernaturally impressed and I was very much moved. She made such an impression on me that I can still see her expression, her gesture, and the very room where she stood. And I shall never lose the memory of it."

The Holy Spirit descended into her soul and undoubtedly showered his gifts on her, as the effects of them were visible to all. But they only reached their maximum splendor when she became a Carmelite.

Preparing for her an inner and not far distant martyrdom, the Spirit of Fortitude would enable her, weak and sensitive by nature, to become strong, magnanimous, heroic. Audacious in desire and in deeds, she would learn to be intrepid, under the guise of simplicity. She would learn to be one of the "little ones," bearing her troubles with a smile, and bearing meekly all suffering.

With the gift of wisdom she would be able to point out to less fortunate souls a new way, a way of salvation, sure, rapid and direct.

And the gift of counsel would enable her to keep in those ways herself, with the Gospels in her hand. His Holiness, Pius XI, attributed to her the gift of holy wisdom "in the exceptional degree." He said that the Spirit of Truth unveiled and made known to her what is very often hidden from sages and learned people, to reveal to the humble and the meek of heart. He called her "Word of God." What greater title could anyone bestow on her?

This great Pontiff, the Vicar of Christ, thus described Theresa and pointed to her soul as an example for all Christians.

Guided by these gifts, Theresa knew how to act. Aided by divine grace, she obtained wonderful answers to prayer—above human understanding and at times without any volition of her own. Without any knowledge of literature or art, she produced a book which is considered a masterpiece of poetry and inspiration.

She painted pictures, which are admitted to be unusual, considering she never had any lessons in either drawing or painting. She had a great love of art as a child and would have given much to have had the chance of developing this talent. M. Martin thought he perceived some artistic talent in Celine and he consulted Marie in Theresa's presence, in regard to having a good master to teach her. He was about to ask Theresa if she would care to join in the lessons (which she was most anxious to do) when Marie intervened with the words: "It would be of no use to Theresa; she has no talent."

Poor little Theresa was silent, and in her love for God she found strength to offer this sacrifice to him.

In her the gift of love would henceforth replace the fear and timidity from which she had suffered ever since her mother died. Love would refine this pure soul that would tolerate nothing that was not pleasing to God. Love such as this does not count the cost of anything earthly and does not measure its actions by any standard. With her, it was "all for Jesus."

Everything inspired her to prayer. She was strong and yet gentle; she abandoned herself entirely to the love of Christ; she reposed on his heart listening to its beats, understanding his desires through the gift of piety. It is a supernatural instinct which comes without learning; it leads the soul to prayer and meditation intuitively, just as the bee sucks nectar and the birds build their nests. Everything uplifted her, everything spurred her on, everything led her to God—the sight of a flower, the beauties of nature—everything.

Toward the end of Theresa's life, when she was very ill, one day she was walking in the garden, leaning on the arm of Sister Agnes (her dear Pauline), when she caught sight of a mother hen gathering all the little chicks under her wing to keep them warm. She looked at them for a moment and then burst out crying.

Questioned about it, she could not reply at once but when back in her cell she explained to Pauline that this gesture of the hen brought vividly to her mind the immense tenderness our Lord has for each one of us, as he once told the multitudes: "As the hen gathers the chicks under her wings, so do I...." And she thought to herself, with great comfort, that she had always kept herself under his sheltering wing.

If she felt the need to put on the armor of the Holy Spirit to fight the good fight, as St. Paul says, and learn how to suffer in silence, she also needed to take refuge under the Virgin Mary's mantle to hide from the world. She was afraid of the world; she feared its praises and its wiles.

On account of her constant headaches, Theresa's father took her away from school and kept her at home. However, she was sent twice a week to a lady for instruction. This lady used to entertain a good deal, often receiving her friends in the very room where Theresa was studying. It was difficult for the child to keep her attention on her lessons. By hearing some of the conversation now and then, she learned many things it would have been better for her not to have known.

In many ways they tried to make her vain by praising her looks, and her beautiful hair, not out of any malice, to be sure, but more because they thought such compliments must surely be pleasing to her.

She began to fear that in her frailty she might entertain a liking for such things. She felt sorry for people whose position in society obliged them to indulge in such frivolities.

Theresa begged to return to school and for permission to join the Children of Mary. She attended their meetings, more to give pleasure to Marie than because she cared about them herself. She never made any friends among the girls. She had nothing in common with them, and as soon as she could she would creep quietly away to the chapel and spend the rest of the time there with her Jesus. It was not that she felt any loneliness of heart. On the contrary, it was because she desired the companionship of Jesus.

She learned the truth of the words she had often heard her father sing:

"This world is my ship but not my abiding home!"

About this time Jesus asked of her a great sacrifice. Marie followed Pauline to Carmel. She thought that by now her little sister had learned enough and was strong enough to stand on her own feet. Poor Theresa, who ran to Marie with all her troubles, felt lost indeed. What should she do without her? In whom could she confide now? Who would guide her along the thorny path? She thought then of her little brothers in heaven, and implored their aid that she be granted peace of soul. Immediately she felt her prayer had been answered and peace inundated her heart.

Marie entered Carmel on October 15, 1886, and took the name of Sister Marie of the Sacred Heart. Thus the year that Theresa lost her dear sister Marie she became a "Child of Mary."

As soon as Theresa heard of Marie's intention to leave home to enter the Order of Carmel she resolved never to seek her own pleasure and then she cried profusely. At that time she was very easily moved to tears, and says of herself: "I cried for big sorrows, but I also cried about the slightest little thing. For instance: I had a great desire to practice virtue in every form. I had never done any manual labor in the house, not even for myself, since Celine cleaned my bedroom. Sometimes *to please God* I would make my own bed. At other times I would bring in all of Celine's pots of flowers and her young plants, as I said, *solely to please God.* Of course I ought not to have bothered my head about thanks from human beings, but, alas! It was not so with me. If Celine did not show pleasure at my little delicate attentions, tears would flow copiously.

"If I had the misfortune at any time to hurt anyone's feelings, even without having had the slightest intention of doing so, instead of at once acknowledging my fault and begging their pardon, I would run away and cry, thus increasing their discomfort rather than diminishing it.

"When I lost my dear Marie's daily counsel, sympathy and guidance, I determined to turn entirely to God for consolation. My soul overflows with gratitude that he gave me strength and courage to conquer myself and gain tranquility of spirit."

Apostle

No longer tormented now with self-examinations, Theresa, having thrown off all such impediments, was free to become a true apostle.

Is it not the preoccupation with self, under all its various forms, that prevents souls from meditation on the Passion of Christ and keeps the number of apostles so low?

Even during childhood, Theresa made efforts to overcome self. She was good to the poor who came to the gate each Monday asking for charity, and to the children who came for instruction.

She would speak of God's goodness to the servants in the house, and she had a special gift for saying things to inspire their zeal. Feeling things very strongly herself, she was enabled to make them see their duty more clearly and to comprehend better the infinite mercy of Jesus.

In thinking of all this in later years she remarked: "I always felt so much compassion for people who had to serve others and were dependent on them." And in referring to the difference between mistress and maid and the gulf between classes she said: "I maintain that this in itself is a proof of the existence of the kingdom of heaven, where everyone will be judged solely on his own merits. The poor and little ones will be well compensated for the many humiliations they have had to endure down here."

She also prepared children for their First Communion, and then came her desire for greater things.

To this ardent and pure soul nothing in life was small or insignificant. In everything she saw the finger of God, which pointed out to her his holy will. One morning, while closing her missal after Mass, she noticed one of the little pictures in it sticking out. It was an image of the crucifixion and the corner that was visible showed just one hand of Christ pierced and dripping blood.

That hand, so mutilated and so little noticed by the world, made a tremendous impression on her and inspired her with new and deeper sentiments. She reflected at what a tremendous price our redemption had been bought and yet so few were at the foot of the cross to do honor to that sacred blood and give back love for love.

From then on she made her resolution to spend her life at the foot of the cross, treasuring that blood shed for us, and helping to apply it to those careless souls who go through life ignoring it.

What a grand mission! This was also the life work of St. Mary Magdalene of Pazzi, of Mother Mary of Jesus, the foundress of the Order of "Victims of the Sacred Heart," and of so very many other saintly souls.

One single drop of the divine Blood, shed with so much love and at the cost of such terrible suffering, would have been sufficient to redeem a thousand worlds and yet it lies in the dust neglected and trodden on! Souls that do not appreciate what Christ has done for them live in sin. Very often such souls die far from God. Yet Christ shed his blood for their salvation.

Before her entrance into Carmel, our Lord gave Theresa a proof of how dear to him was her resolve to apply to sinners all the merits of his Passion and he showed it to her in a most touching manner.

Early in June, 1889, there was a great commotion in France over the brutal murder of two women and a child which had taken place in Paris. The time for the assassin's execution was approaching, but the culprit showed not the slightest sign of repentance, and he firmly refused all spiritual help.

Theresa Martin felt an indescribable sorrow...to die on the gallows and then to face an eternity of punishment! She felt she must save that soul, and yet she was only a girl of fifteen, far away from the murderer and with no power or influence.

She set herself to apply to this wandering soul all the merits of the Sacred Passion, offering them unceasingly to God the Father for the salvation of this unfortunate sinner.

She never had any doubt that her prayer would be answered. In her simple, confident way she told Jesus so, but asked that "as he was her very first sinner" he give her a sign, any little sign, so that she would know that her prayers had been answered.

M. Martin was in the habit of relating to his daughters the news of the day, as he did not permit them to read the papers. In this exceptional case, however, Theresa did not think she would be doing wrong if she just glanced at the Catholic Gazette, called *La Croix,* to find the sign she asked of God. In this issue of that paper for September 1, 1889, she found that her request had been granted.

When the prisoner was taken to the court he was delivered into the hands of the executioner. Deibler and his assistants were already there waiting to perform their duty. At two minutes to five, while the birds were singing their evening song, the word of command rang out: "Present arms."

The prison door opened and the assassin, livid of face, appeared on the threshold.

The chaplain stood between the prisoner and the scaffold in order to prevent the sight of it to the poor wretch as long as possible; but the criminal pushed aside both priest and executioner.

He faced the guillotine....

Deibler seized him none too gently and with his attendants forced the man's head in the "lunette" under the raised blade.... At that moment a change came over the face of the man, his lips moved and he was heard to utter the word: "Crucifix." The chaplain approached and put it to the unfortunate man's lips. He kissed it three times, with evident sorrow and contrition.

This was the article Theresa read in *La Croix*. She felt she could hardly bear it. She fled to her room, for her tears of joy would have betrayed her.

She had asked for a sign from heaven, and she had received one which surpassed her expectations. Through the Precious Blood of our Savior had come to her this thirst for souls. It had been on the very wounds of our divine Redeemer that this, her first rescued soul, had placed his lips at the very last moment of his life.

It was almost too much for her overflowing heart. From that day she constantly heard in the depths of her soul that *"I thirst"* from the agonizing Christ on the cross, and the more she tried to quench that thirst the more she acquired it herself.

It was a veritable interchange of love: she offered to souls the blood of Christ, and to Christ she offered those souls regenerated in that same blood.

Theresa never forsook the assassin. When she was a Carmelite and anyone gave her alms, she would ask the mother prioress if some of it could not be applied to the suffrage of that soul which, to all appearances, needed help so badly.

Isn't this a lesson for all of us? Our dear dead perhaps languish in purgatory and we so soon forget them and abandon them to their fate, not remembering that between earth and heaven there is such a thing as expiation. While God is infinitely just, it is possible for us by our prayers, good works and sufferings, and through the Holy Sacrifice of the Mass offered for the Poor Souls, to obtain their release from purgatory. Are we doing all we can for them?

"Listen, Daughter!"

Where could Theresa best follow her activities as an apostle? Where could she quench this thirst for souls and cooperate for their salvation?

These were questions she earnestly asked herself and she considered all the various vocations with a view to selecting the one which best suited her purpose. Missionaries, hospitalers, helpers of priests in parish work—she passed them all in mental review and found good in each one.

But an inner voice seemed to remind her that the way of life where incessant prayer is united to constant mortification, an immolation that carries with it surrender, must be the vocation that will more completely satisfy the *Sitio* of the divine Redeemer—the Carmelite vocation...in a word, the vocation of Marie and Pauline.

Theresa thought that it was harder for human nature to work without seeking the result of its labor and without any sense of discouragement; that to work against one's very self is the most difficult of all; that this dying to self is more fruitful than any other for obtaining the salvation of souls; and that the goal in entering Carmel was essentially to pray for priests and make an immolation of herself for the needs of the Church. Therefore, this was the work Theresa wished to undertake, seeking to imprison herself, as soon as possible, so as to earn for souls the Beatific Vision.

Without any human encouragement, without even the help of a spiritual director, she followed the maxim of St. John of the Cross, inasmuch as he was known to have said: "The least little movement of pure love is more helpful to the Church than all good works put together." This was Theresa's directing principle throughout her life. She resolved, therefore, to go where she would have more to give, first, to God, and then, indirectly but equally as effective, to her neighbor.

The first germ of her vocation, however, came to her as a child; when Pauline announced her intention of forsaking the world to enter the Carmelite Order, Theresa at once said firmly: "Then I will be a nun, too."

An older sister, who is away at school for most of the year, appearing only at holiday time, acquires glamour, something for little ones to look up to and try to emulate. Theresa thought all the world of Pauline. If asked soon after she had learned to talk, what she was thinking of, she would say: "Pauline."

So it is little wonder that when she heard of Pauline's vocation she determined to imitate her, although the words did not convey much to her youthful mind.

After Pauline entered Carmel she described as well as she could the life of the convent; she pictured for Theresa the cloister with its austerities and self-denials. She then more profoundly tried to explain to her young sister the infinite sweetness of a soul united with the Divine Master, and especially of those elect souls who have given up everything in life for him.

Theresa kept all these things in her heart, searching therein for future light. One evening she was given to understand with great clarity of vision that Carmel was in reality that faraway desert she dreamed of so much as a child, when she so longed to be an anchorite and leave the world to meditate on God in peace and quiet.

No trace of doubt remained in her mind that she had at last found what her soul craved. With the love she had for souls, and the urge she felt to give herself for them more and more, she decided then and there to enter Carmel as soon as possible. This was before her fifteenth birthday, an age when young girls are full of romance and enthusiasm.

If only she could enter at Christmas—the anniversary of what she called "her conversion"!

Celine, too, had felt the call to Carmel, and the two spent many happy hours up in the belvedere, discussing their vocation: the Carmelite life and the bliss of the Beatific Vision.

"We were full of faith and hope," she says, "and charity enabled us to find on earth, him whom we had been seeking. These spiritual conversations were destined to bear fruit and the practice of virtue became natural and sweet to me. At first I may have shown traces of the struggle in my face, but as time went on I began to find it easier to give up things."

Jesus said, "To him that has, more shall be given." And Theresa admitted that, "For one grace faithfully received he gave me many others.

"Jesus saw my desire, and inspired my confessor to allow me to increase the frequency of my Communions, and for this I was full of joy. Jesus does not come down from heaven just to stay in the ciborium. He comes down each day from heaven to find another heaven, in each soul loving him and where he is pleased to reign."

Heroic Consent

Between Theresa and Carmel though, there existed a barrier which, humanly speaking, seemed insurmountable: her aged father.

Theresa trembled at the very thought of breaking the news to him and asking of him the supreme sacrifice. He was sixty-four years of age and in very poor health.

One who has already had one stroke expects another to follow sooner or later. M. Martin had already undergone his preliminary one. In addition, while fishing one day he had been stung in the neck by a poisonous insect and the wound had not yielded to any of the remedies tried.

Was Theresa to leave her old and infirm father, she, the little Queen of his heart? What a battle raged in her heart and her senses!

Months were passing quickly and Christmas was approaching. It seemed to her that our Lord was calling more and more strongly, and the poor little queen was afraid to speak.

Pentecost is a feast of light, strength and joy, which prepares the soul for martyrdom. Theresa chose that day as the most appropriate one for her revelation. In the morning she prayed most fervently to the Holy Spirit. She implored the help of the holy Apostles who overcame their

timidity and weakness and became strong and magnanimous. Strengthened by the breath of this same Holy Spirit she made up her mind to speak that evening.

The scene was a very moving one and Celine, who was
the only one who received true enlightenment on it, describes it with the mind and pen of an artist. The father had
just come back from vespers. He was tired and stopped
to sit on a bench in the garden before going into the house.
His face shown with a spiritual radiance. With his hands
folded, as if in prayer, he revealed the great peace and joy
that pervaded his soul lost in contemplation.

It was a delightful evening and he admired the beauty
of nature all around him, aglow in the rays of the setting
sun. The birds flying about and singing their evening
hymn to their Creator bade farewell to the dying day.

Theresa, looking at her father's serene face, felt her courage almost failing. Was she to be the one to disturb that
serenity and bring sorrow in its place?

She felt the unbidden tears rising to her eyes. With a
silent cry for help from heaven, she very quietly went to
sit by her father.

Poor child! She saw, she felt his look upon her seeking
for the cause of her tears. He took her hands and placed
them on his heart: "What troubles you, my little queen?
Confide in me." And drawing her tenderly within his arm
he gently led her into the garden where they walked up
and down. Thus it was that she told him quite simply that
she wished to enter Carmel at the age of fifteen.

The first shock was terrible to this frail, old man. He saw
in an instant his lonely fireplace, his empty home, and the
loneliness of his old age. Above all, he felt that Theresa,
the apple of his eye and queen of his heart, was abandoning him, and his heart was broken. He wept. This was a
tribute to nature only, for of course, he never intended to
go against her wishes. At the same time he thought she

was too young, and should wait a while. He was really only half-hearted in these requests. Then his fine nature, as a good Christian, reasserted itself, and he remembered his young wife's most earnest prayer: "God, give me many children that I may consecrate them all to you." He was very soon convinced by the calm and simple reasoning of his beloved daughter, and promised to help her to the best of his ability.

Perceiving a little white flower growing in the crevices of the garden wall, he plucked it, root and all, and offered it to Theresa telling her that God had planted it there through love, and had tended it carefully through good and bad weather and brought it to maturity, just as he had done in her case. Both the father and daughter saw a symbol of her own life in the story of the "little flower," as he liked to think of her. That is why he depicted this little parable with the heart of a poet.

Theresa took her little plant with her to Carmel, where she kept it in her copy of *The Imitation of Christ*. Curiously enough, when she was approaching death she noted in her writings that its bloom had a broken stalk quite near the root, and she saw in that a sign that her end, too, was very near.

Difficulties

Among the many difficulties to be surmounted, the worst one had been overcome by the heroic virtue of M. Martin.

M. Guerin, Theresa's uncle, had also to be consulted, in view of the fact that he had been appointed guardian to the children on the death of their mother.

He was opposed to the whole idea and called it folly even to talk of a girl of fifteen entering an austere order like that of the Carmelites. It was against all human prudence and would raise such a storm of criticism that all France would be up in arms.

Theresa cried. M. Martin espoused her cause with all the eloquence of which he was capable and which astounded his brother-in-law although it did not make him alter his decision. In fact, M. Guerin declared that nothing short of a miracle would make him give his consent.

Theresa, as was her usual habit, abandoned herself to prayer, but when this determination was kept up for three days she felt as if she were indeed forsaken by heaven and earth. She tells us that she felt as if she were lost, and that she understood quite well what our Lady and St. Joseph felt on those terrible three days when they searched in vain for the Divine Child Jesus. "I seemed to be lost in a wild forest alone," she said, "or rather, like a frail barque in a tempest, tossed about with no mariner at the helm. Jesus was there in the boat, but he was asleep and did not seem to hear my voice. I could not see my way, the darkness was impenetrable, a veritable death.

"All nature seemed to take part in this engulfing sadness, for the sun did not show a single gleam in those troubled days and the rain came down incessantly. So I had often noticed that nature matched her moods with mine. When I wept the heavens wept with me. When I had cause to rejoice the blue of the firmament had never a cloud in it."

On the fourth day after her announcement to her father, she went to see her uncle. What was her astonishment and joy when he received her with open arms, his manner completely changed! Kissing her with paternal tenderness, he exclaimed: "The miracle is no longer necessary. I prayed to our Lord to change my heart and make me see your point of view and he did so. And now I say to you: go in peace, dear child. You are a privileged little flower that the Lord wishes to pluck for himself and I would not be the one to oppose him."

And so the second obstacle was removed.

Now Carmel must consent.

Marie (Sister Marie of the Sacred Heart) thought it rather imprudent for Theresa to enter so young. Pauline was on Theresa's side and had always been. In fact she had suggested years before that Theresa should confide her wishes and hopes to the mother prioress, Mother Marie Gonzaga.

The latter, though kind, had taken the matter seriously but answered, and with good reason, that she could scarcely accept as a postulant a child of nine, as Theresa was then. Now, however, she was quite eager to admit Theresa.

Many of the other nuns opposed her entry but the greatest of these oppositions came from Monsignor Delatroette, superior of the Carmel of Lisieux, a hard and austere man. The mother prioress tried to move him, but without success. She then tried the foundress of the Carmel of Lisieux, Mother Genevieve of St. Theresa. This saintly and very sweet woman, confined in the infirmary by age and many infirmities, was well pleased to plead Theresa's cause, but it would have been better had she never attempted it. The inflexible superior's patience gave way entirely and he spoke very strongly and with a good deal of ill feeling, refusing to give further consideration to Theresa's application for the time being.

After such opposition, who would have dared to enter into further argument?

Theresa, although generally shy, dared to approach him. She went with her father, but received only a refusal, so there was nothing more to be said. "However," the Monsignor added, "I am only the mouthpiece of his Lordship the Bishop. If he chooses to give you the desired permission, I shall have nothing to add."

As the drowning man clutches even at a straw, Theresa, in her desperation, saw in these few words a ray of light and hope.

So on October 13, 1887, she ventured to the episcopal palace at Bayeux. Fearfully she crossed the threshold of the palace, where she met the vicar general, Monsignor Reverony, who showed great surprise at her having an audience. He seemed not too favorably disposed toward her admission. Seated on the edge of a large chair, Theresa unfolded her great desire with all the eloquence she could command. Then, as she rose, she felt unable to speak and simply looked at him with eyes full of tears. "Oh," exclaimed the vicar general, "I see diamonds shining, but don't let his Lordship see them!"

Theresa had put her hair up for the first time, hoping fondly that this act of hers would add many more years to her age, and it did in a way. But no one, seeing that angelic child with golden curls tumbling all round her shoulders could possibly have taken her for a strong-minded, determined young woman.

She had hoped that her father would speak for her, but he let her explain her own mission. Gathering up her courage, she made her statement.

"Since when have you had a vocation?" asked the bishop, Monsignor Hugonin.

"Oh! a very long time, your Lordship," Theresa replied.

"Come, come, it can't be as much as fifteen years," interrupted the vicar general laughing.

"No, but you can subtract only a few years, because I have desired to give myself to God since the age of three," she added.

Thinking to please M. Martin, the bishop tried to induce Theresa to give up the idea altogether. He was surprised when her father most ardently supported her and stated that if his Excellency would not give his consent, he would take Theresa on the diocesan pilgrimage to Rome, where he would not hesitate to enlist the services of the Holy Father himself on her behalf.

Before deciding, the bishop said he must consult Monsignor Delatroette.

When Theresa heard the name of her most determined enemy, she gave up all hope of the bishop's cooperation. She cared not whether the bishop disliked "diamonds" or not. She treated him to a whole cascade of them and wept unrestrainedly.

Good Monsignor Hugonin was quite upset at her disappointment and put his hands on her head, as if she were indeed a child, and said: "All is not lost. I am glad you are going to Rome with your dear father. Perhaps it will even strengthen your vocation. Instead of crying, you ought to rejoice." He promised to send her an answer which might possibly reach her in Italy. He accompanied her to the door and gave her his blessing.

In Rome

It was night when they reached Rome. Theresa was asleep, and was awakened by the porters calling: "Roma!" Her heart beat with excitement at finding herself at last in the Eternal City—that city where the Pope resides. It was from Pope Leo XIII that she hoped for a realization of her desire.

It was only three days after her journey to Bayeux that they started from Lisieux on November 4, to join, in Paris, the pilgrimage which was going to be solemnly consecrated in the Church of the Sacred Heart at Montmartre. They left Paris on November 7. She was traveling, not knowing where, and yet she felt that great things were going to happen to her. One thing she had truly loved in the French capital, and that was their visit to the Church of Our Lady of Victories. It was to our dear Blessed Lady, under that title, that Theresa owed the miracle of her cure when she was a little girl. There was the same statue, only larger than the one in her bedroom, that had smiled at her when she was restored to health. She now implored this same Mother of God to obtain for her her heart's desire, and to keep her from evil all the days of her life.

The journey through Switzerland was beautiful and picturesque, with its high mountain peaks covered with snow, and its deep valleys filled with giant ferns and purple heather. In the valley's green grass lay peaceful lakes and little smiling villages looking almost like toys placed there by the careless hand of a child.

Whether it was valley or mountain, meadow or lake, it was all beauty, and it made a great impression on Theresa, who was seeing it all for the first time. She tried to impress it on her memory for the future while she sang a paean of joy in her heart to the Creator of such wonders. She knew that some day all this scenery would be but a memory, that it would help her to think little or nothing of the trivialities that daily beset her path, and that it would enable her to turn and love God more, since he has made our exile so beautiful to behold. Theresa realized that we are not to attach ourselves to these fleeting shadows, since we are told that our hearts cannot imagine what God has in store for those who love him.

From Switzerland the train took them through the plains of Lombardy to Milan, where she was impressed by the grand Cathedral. Venice left her rather depressed because of its gruesome prisons, where thousands of unfortunate people were left to languish and die, some of whom no doubt were innocent. She admired the magnificent monuments, St. Mark's, the Doges' Palace and all the beautiful palaces flanking the Grand Canal, "all solemn and so wonderfully silent." She found Venice attractive, but too sad.

In Padua she admired Donatello's wonderful sculptures, especially those on the tomb of Saint Anthony, whom she venerated.

In Bologna more art treasures interested her, but above all, the church where the body of St. Catherine rests. Her face still bears the impress of the kiss bestowed on her by the Infant Jesus.

They visited Loreto, where Theresa felt great joy over the "Holy House." She had the great happiness of receiving Holy Communion on the very spot where the Angel

Gabriel appeared to the Blessed Virgin Mary and announced that she would be the Mother of the Savior, and where Jesus lived until he was thirty years old. Many miracles have taken place there and everything speaks eloquently of the poverty of the Holy Family and the simplicity of their mode of living.

Theresa said concerning her visit to Loreto: "Everything is poor, simple and primitive. The women still wear the graceful dress of the country and have not, as in the large towns, adopted the modern Paris fashions. I found Loreto enchanting. And what shall I say of the Holy House? I was overwhelmed with emotion when I realized that I was under the very roof that had sheltered the Holy Family. I gazed on the same wall our Lord had looked on. I trod the ground once moistened with the sweat of St. Joseph's toil, and saw the little chamber of the Annunciation, where the Blessed Virgin Mary held Jesus in her arms after she had borne him there in her virginal womb. I even put my Rosary into the little porringer used by the Divine Child. How sweet those memories!

"I shall never forget the great joy I experienced in receiving Holy Communion there, and words fail me to describe it. What will it be like in the kingdom of God, when we shall be able to speak to him face to face?

"He likes to leave us this little house to show us his poverty that we may imitate it and his hidden life, and later on merit to come and share his glory in the palace of his infinite splendor."

In Rome, three things greatly attracted Theresa: the Vatican, the Colosseum, and the Catacombs. In the Colosseum she knelt reverently in the dust of the arena where so many holy martyrs were put to a gruesome death. There, where so many heroes gave their lives for Christ, Theresa asked martyrdom for herself, and she felt that it would be granted her.

The Catacombs aroused in her lively feelings of faith and edification. She was especially attracted by St. Cecilia because of her unswerving faith in God, and the singular grace accorded her to be able to recall to purity those who had become careless in the practice of this virtue.

St. Agnes' Basilica pleased her immensely, and she tells us that Jesus gave her a special little favor like fond parents bestow on their much-loved children.

Theresa craved a relic of St. Agnes to be able to give to her dear Sister Agnes. She was unable to obtain it at the basilica, and no one knew where one could be procured. Heaven came to her aid. A little square of red mosaic detached itself from the ceiling over St. Agnes tomb and fell at Theresa's feet. She picked it up with veneration and love. The mosaic is a very ancient one and goes back to the time of the young saint's death.

Then the Vatican!

Theresa looked forward to seeing many things in Rome, but above all she desired to see Pope Leo XIII. She wanted to meet him and yet she dreaded to do so. She knew that on him depended all the hopes of her vocation, because no letter had come from Monsignor Hugonin and the Holy Father's consent was her only hope.

To obtain the great grace she wanted, she would have to ask for it in front of cardinals, archbishops and bishops. The very thought of daring to speak to the Pope made her tremble.

The pilgrims had all been bidden to the Vatican on the morning of November 20, to assist at the Pope's Mass and to be received in audience by him afterwards. At eight o'clock, Leo XIII entered the Sistine Chapel, silently blessed those assembled, and knelt to make his preparation for the Holy Sacrifice. Pope Leo XIII, pale and thin, was the true figure of an ascetic, but even more so when he closed his eyes in prayer and his lids hid his piercing black eyes, which spoke so eloquently of his genius.

His preparation at an end, he arose and vested. His thin, tall figure was rather bent, and his hand trembled slightly as he rested it on the arm of one of his chamberlains to go up the steps of the altar.

Monsignor Laveille, who was one of the many privileged ones to assist with Theresa and many others at the Pope's Mass, said of Leo XIII: "It is better than any sermon to see his Holiness at the altar. His words are slow and clear, and what faith! What tender devotion in the tone of his voice, in his manner, and in the least of his actions. Above all, what piety in the final prayers he himself composed and prescribed to the faithful throughout the world!"

To Theresa, Leo XIII seemed in very truth a Holy Father. After a Mass of thanksgiving, said by one of the chamberlains, they were admitted to the audience chamber, and Theresa felt impelled to talk to him as a daughter to a beloved father.

The first to be received were the pilgrims from Coutances, then those from Bayeux and finally those from Nantes.

To everyone's satisfaction, Monsignor Germain, Bishop of Coutances, presented each one of his children separately for the special blessing, announcing their name and status and title. To each one the Holy Father spoke a few words in a fatherly tone, blessing them cordially, and presenting each with a commemorative medal.

The Bayeux pilgrims were not nearly so fortunate. The Abbot Reverony had not the charm or grace of manners of Monsignor Germain, and he was more concerned that the strict discipline of the court be kept.

When he saw the two Martin sisters approaching the Holy Father with calm, resolute faces, he feared that Theresa was going to implore a favor, so he raised his voice and absolutely forbade anyone to address the Pope.

This momentarily frustrated Theresa's hopes. She cast

a despairing look in Celine's direction. Not for nothing was she called "Celine the intrepid." She replied: "Speak."

Theresa no longer hesitated; she knelt at the feet of the sovereign Pontiff and kissed his foot. He held out his hand and she said: "Most Holy Father, I have a great favor to ask of you."

The Pope inclined his head and fixed his piercing black eyes on hers as if to read her very soul. Theresa spoke: "Holy Father, in honor of your Jubilee, will you allow me to enter Carmel when I am fifteen?" This was just what the vicar general had feared, and without giving the Pope time to reply, he interrupted: "Holy Father, this is a child who desires to become a Carmelite, but the superiors of the Carmel are looking into the matter." "Well, my child," said His Holiness, "do whatever the superiors decide."

Theresa clasped her hands and rested them on his knee and made a final effort: "Holy Father, if only you would say 'yes,' everyone else would agree."

The Holy Father looked at her "fixedly," and clearly and emphatically replied: "Well, well! You will enter if it is God's will."

Theresa was opening her mouth to speak again, when two noble guards and Monsignor Reverony lifted her to her feet, but before she was led away the Pope gently placed his hand on her lips to enjoin silence and then lifted it to bless her.

M. Martin fared better at the audience than his daughter. The vicar general showed himself very amiable when his turn came, and presented him as the father of two Carmelites. Leo XIII put his hand on the venerable head and gave him a special blessing in Christ's name.

Pope Leo XIII was the first Pope who had anything to do with Theresa, and his action was preparatory, his language prophetic, even though it sounded evasive...."If it be God's will." God did will it, and Theresa entered Carmel at the age of fifteen.

Three more Pontiffs would be concerned with this child: Pius X, who permitted the beginning of the process of canonization; Benedict XV, who issued the decree of her heroic virtues; and Pius XI, who beatified and canonized her, thus inscribing her among the number of saints forever.

But for the moment, poor child! It looked as if she had accomplished nothing, and her father on rejoining her after the audience found her bathed in tears. It was really a trial that little Jesus had sent to her to prove her generosity of soul, since she had offered herself to him to be his little plaything, to do with as he pleased.

On that November day the skies were gray also and the heavy rain mingled with Theresa's tears. Nature's mood and hers coincided once again. All the pilgrims were discussing the "little Carmelite" and looked at her with sympathy. For her, however, all joy in the pilgrimage had been taken away. She saw everything through a mist of tears.

Pompeii, that ancient city which vanished in a moment, its population tragically swallowed up in a stream of red hot lava, looked to her like a story of her life. She would have liked to have found herself alone amid those ruins meditating on the demolition of human hopes, the brevity of life and the vanity of earthly greatness, but she could not. With such a large pilgrimage it was impossible to get away from the others, and there was no chance for meditation.

At Naples they visited the Carthusian Monastery of St. Martino. The horses drawing the carriage in which Theresa and Celine were riding, became frightened and ran away, and the two girls had a narrow escape from death.

Notwithstanding the magnificent view of the bay, Theresa felt she desired nothing more than to return to Lisieux. Until her visit to Rome she had been sustained by a great hope. Having lost that hope she longed to return home to see if there might be a letter for her from Monsignor Hugonin. At Assisi she sought for traces of the "Poverello." Monsignor Reverony, seeing her dejection, was now very kind to her and endeavored to raise her spirits by promising to try to further her cause on his return, but she had lost all confidence in people and gave little value to his promise. She found great consolation, nevertheless, in confiding her troubles to St. Mary Magdalene of Pazzi, the Seraph of Carmel, whose body, beautiful and incorrupt, although somewhat darkened with age, lies under the altar in the choir of the Carmelite Church just outside Florence. Praying at her shrine, Theresa felt strangely comforted, and a little incident, insignificant in itself, served to make her happy:

The pilgrims wanted to touch with their rosaries and medals the crystal case where the saint's body reposes, but Theresa's hand was the only one small enough to get between the bars, so she performed this service for everyone with much pleasure.

They traveled on to Pisa, and thence to Genoa and the enchanting Riviera, which is like a bit of heaven fallen to earth; then to Marseilles, where the magnificent church and bronze statue of the Blessed Virgin and Child, catching the rays of the sun from dawn to sunset, dominate the harbor from on high and can be seen for miles.

Finally, they reached the very beautiful cathedral at Lyons, Our Lady of Fourviere, where the pilgrimage ended and all the travelers separated. On December 2, Theresa returned to Lisieux. This pilgrimage, which started under such happy auspices, ended for her with a bitter disillusionment about all her dearest and most ardently cherished hopes.

Theresa's first visit on her return home was to Pauline, her dear sister at Carmel. She poured out her whole heart and soul to her, and Pauline consoled her as best she could.

She told Theresa to write again to Monsignor Reverony and remind him of his promise. She did this at once and, with the eagerness of a child, expected an answer by return mail, but the days passed and no reply was received. Meanwhile, the beautiful feast of Christmas, always so dear to the heart of a Carmelite, was passing and the Infant Jesus was still sleeping and not heeding his poor "little toy," not even casting a glance at it! This trial was a great one for Theresa, but he whose heart never sleeps taught her that, for one who has faith even as small as a grain of mustard seed, he will perform miracles so as to strengthen that little faith; but to those generous souls who love him, he is not so bountiful, preferring each time to test their faith to the limit.

Did not Jesus let Lazarus die, when informed by his sisters of his illness? At the marriage of Cana when our Blessed Lady pleaded for the host he said: "My hour has not yet come." Yet how quickly he relented, and what miracles then! Lazarus came back from the dead; water was changed into wine...and thus did her Beloved deal with little Theresa. After having tried her for a very long time, he then showered his gifts upon her, granting her heart's desire. However, before being able to accomplish it she had other trials to endure. If things are really worth having they are worth striving for, and this child, mature beyond her years, came to this conclusion after much prayer and meditation.

The Lesson Learned

What were the things Theresa had learned on this long journey?

She had understood the words of the *Imitation of Christ:* Do not run after the shadow of a great name, or seek the greatness of earthly things. Of what use are titles or coats of arms? What lasting good can come from all the modern luxury in the splendid hotels where they stayed during the travels?

All seemed to her vanity and affliction of spirit. She saw that true grandeur consists not in bearing a noble name, but in the quality of the soul.

What a living example of grandeur was her father who, lacking titles, money or nobility was, nevertheless, armed with a lively faith, coupled with ardent piety and generous pardon for all who offended him. Even on their pilgrimage the little pinpricks of life were not lacking.

Another incident served to make Theresa understand the very special apostolic aim of the life in Carmel; namely, prayer for priests, from whom we receive many spiritual benefits, from whom we expect so much, and yet we seldom remember to pray for them.

Their sublime mission does not confirm them in grace. They have to live their lives like ordinary mortals under tremendous difficulties. They have to carry high their standard of faith in the darkness of a world becoming more and more pagan, and keep their hearts pure amid so much corruption. They are in constant awareness of human sinfulness because of their encounters with it in the Sacrament of Penance. This is what we are very often liable to forget.

Theresa in her youth and innocence had created for herself an illusion that all priests were angels from heaven. This late pilgrimage, which included a number of priests, many good and some very holy ones, revealed to her after daily contact with them that some of them were far from perfect.

Theresa did not condemn them, as some people in the world might have done. She pitied them and loved them all the more, feeling a greater desire than ever to pray for them, to make sacrifices for them so as to draw down upon their souls, light, grace and comfort.

How we hope that from heaven St. Theresa will let fall a shower of roses in the guise of a clarion call to prayer for these sacerdotal souls, coupled with a greater sympathy for them in their failings and above all, a great respect for all of them since their lives are consecrated to God.

While in Rome Theresa's faith was strengthened.

In the Colosseum she had sensed the thirst for martyrdom. There also she had learned that all our hope must be built on God only, because we can expect nothing from creatures, since they are feeble and unreliable and can do nothing themselves unless God permits it. Consequently, she said in her heart from that time: "God alone."

Rome likewise made her understand that real happiness comes not from the things that surround us, but that it resides in the center of the soul, where one can build a prison or a palace.

Her soul was flooded with gratitude toward our Lady and St. Joseph, who had taken such care of her on the long journey. When in Paris at the start of the pilgrimage, she asked them both to guard the innocence of her mind and heart. She realized that often in art galleries she would be confronted with pagan art that might generate in her evil thoughts, a thing she had never been guilty of up to that time. She prayed especially for this grace in the Church of Our Lady of Victories in Paris.

Her prayer was granted, and in spite of the many sights which might have disturbed the peace of her soul, she saw none of them and returned unsullied.

A disturbing little incident, however, did occur at the Bologna station on her way home. As the pilgrims descended from the train they found themselves surrounded by young university students, noisy and generally out for a good time. Taking advantage of the tumult and confusion, one of the youths stood before Theresa, stared at her rudely and appraised her from head to foot. Then seizing her in his arms he carried her to the other side of the platform. She sent an agonized, frightened prayer to Mary, our Mother, and then quietly looked at her aggressor without saying a word. He became, as it were, transfixed, looked thoroughly ashamed of himself and moved away in confusion.

A far more subtle temptation assailed her during the pilgrimage.

A young pilgrim, handsome and from a good family, fell in love with her and paid her a lot of attention. Theresa answered him with cold reserve, her only defense against his advances. She confided this experience to Celine but to no one else.

"Oh!" she said, "it is time Jesus would take me away from the poisoned air of the world. I can see that my heart is weak enough to be easily attracted by love from creatures, and like many others might succumb also. Every creature has its weakness, and I am as weak as any of them."

This, then, was the secret of Theresa's victory: her entire trust in God's help, and the humble opinion of her own efforts.

Sister Marie Agnes remarked: "One only had to see this young servant of God to be convinced of her purity.... She seemed as if surrounded by innocence, and although she revealed to me that never in her life had she had any temptation against purity, she nevertheless exercised the greatest vigilance to keep to the end the integrity of her treasure."

"The pure in heart are often crowned with thorns," Theresa wrote one day, as a Carmelite, to a young friend living in the world. "Lilies think they have lost their whiteness and imagine that the thorns have pierced their corolla, but lilies amid the thorns are Jesus' special predilection. Blessed are those who have suffered temptation and withstood it."

With great hope in her heart Theresa prepared during the following months for the high standard of life she had chosen for herself, and very wisely began by constantly performing little acts of virtue. All of them were acts against her own will which she had resolved to conquer at all costs.

She trained herself to silence when she felt she would have liked to speak. She performed many little acts of kindness to those around her, without drawing attention to them or expecting any thanks. Thus she laid a true and lasting foundation to her life of sanctity.

Farewell

"For my New Year's present in 1888, Jesus again sent me his cross. Mother Marie Gonzaga wrote to me that she had received a letter from Monsignor Hugonin, Bishop of Bayeux, on December 28, giving his consent to my entry in Carmel immediately, but that she had decided not to permit me to enter the convent until after Lent." Theresa was overwhelmed by this fresh disappointment. She saw her worldly ties broken, because she had given up everything for her vocation, and yet this holy ark of refuge kept on denying admittance to the poor little dove seeking shelter.

The "fiat" had gone forth and there was no argument possible. April 9 was the day chosen for her entrance.

Monsignor Reverony had been favorably impressed by the sincerity and maturity of her conduct during the pilgrimage. He was even pleased with the frank audacity she displayed in speaking to the Pope in spite of his express command to the contrary. It showed him that she had courage, energy, and constancy, virtues that made her choose without hesitation the hard life of a Carmelite.

That he observed her every moment of the pilgrimage is a known fact. He wanted to be quite sure of the caliber of this embryo Carmelite. Perhaps it was he himself who made the favorable report to the Bishop in her behalf. At

Assisi he promised to do his best to assist her, and in Lisieux he fulfilled that promise.

Unfortunately for Theresa's ardent hopes, the mother prioress deemed it wise to wait until Easter. This was partly not to offend Monsignor Delatroette, who was still obdurate, and partly not to expose this very young girl to all the rigors of a Carmelite Lent so soon after her entry.

This setback nearly caused Theresa to relax in her mortifications. But like other temptations, she was able to overcome it, and she redoubled her efforts and continued to offer Jesus her little sacrifices.

April 8 was her last day at home, a very painful and sad one. Nothing, in fact, can be sadder to any creature called by God to follow him, than this last good-bye to a loved family and home, where every nook and corner holds many dear memories of one's childhood.

One would wish to be ignored, to leave unobserved. On the contrary, the usual affection is intensified and everyone shows special attention. It is then that one is filled with anguish and becomes numb with suffering. All has been said, and one would weep if one spoke. For the last time the old walnut table saw them all gathered together around this festive board. The two families of Martin and Guerin were there to bid farewell to the little Theresa whom they all loved so dearly and who held the place of honor in their hearts.

All agreed that they would accompany her to Carmel the following morning. They would assist at Mass there and receive Holy Communion.

Leonie wrote: "I was amazed at the strength of soul shown by Theresa. She was the only one who was perfectly calm. I told her to think well before she entered a religious order, adding, that from my own experience [Leonie had joined the Poor Clares and had to leave because of poor health], I realized that one needs very good health to lead a life entailing great and daily sacrifices, and such a life was not to be undertaken lightly or without very serious consideration. Her answer to me was a smile, radiant with joy, showing me that she was ready for any sacrifice and accepted it with happiness."

In fact, Theresa's ardor was not a transient glow, nor her desire merely a romantic idea. She wasn't entering Carmel to search for spiritual consolations and comforts—she could have had these in abundance in the bosom of her family. She was going to dwell in Carmel to lead a life of sacrifice and voluntary sufferings, to immolate herself in expiation for the sins of others, and above all, to be of very special help to priests. After one last glance around her dear home, Les Buissonnets, the happy nest of her childhood, the little group wended its way to the convent.

At Mass after the Communion, Theresa heard nothing but sobs all around her. It was the supreme moment of her oblation. She alone was dry eyed. When Mass was ended, she was the first to rise and go to the door of the cloister. "My heart was beating to suffocation and I felt like dying," she said later. "What a moment of indescribable agony. Only those who have been through the same will know what it was like."

She turned and kissed each in turn, and then knelt in front of her father for his blessing. He, too, knelt there with tears streaming down his face and blessed her, his little queen, the flower of his flock. Of his feelings when the door opened to admit and shelter this much loved daughter of his, still scarcely more than a child—a few months past fifteen—no one can write. Only God knows what her father suffered in his heart.

Monsignor Delatroette in a tactless speech to the mother prioress and the assembled community said: "Well, Reverend Sisters, sing if you wish the 'Te Deum.' As the bishop's delegate I present to you this child of fifteen that you wished so much to have. I wish you the fulfillment of your hopes and that you will not suffer disillusionment. As for the rest, let me remind you that her entry was quite against my wishes, and therefore, the responsibility is entirely yours!"

He astounded the whole community with his words and wounded the heart of the sorely stricken father, but he in no way disturbed the soul of Theresa, which was given up to suffering.

It was her first public humiliation and the first link in a long chain. Because her reason for entering Carmel was "to save souls and especially to pray for priests," it was necessary for her to adopt the means in order to attain the end. Our Lord let her understand that it was by the cross that he would give her souls. The more crosses she met with, the stronger grew her attraction to suffering. This was Theresa's way for five years, but she tells us: "I alone knew it. This was precisely the flower I wished to offer to Jesus, a hidden flower which keeps its perfume only for heaven."

This young girl entered the convent with a calm and dignity that impressed every one of the beholders. "The Mothers who had expected to see a child were filled with great respect in her presence, admiring her self-restraint and simple manner," wrote Mother Agnes. "One of them, Sister St. John of the Cross, who had been strongest in her opposition against the entry of one so young, told me later: 'I thought that you would soon have cause to regret having labored so hard to give your little sister to the Order, saying to myself, what disappointments and what disillusionments will she not suffer before long, but indeed, it was I who was mistaken. Sister Theresa of the Infant Jesus is extraordinary!'"

Theresa loved everything in the convent. She thought all things were beautiful, even her bare, tiny cell. Now she

really had found the anchorite desert of her dreams, and
with thankfulness and joy exclaimed even on the first day:
"Here I am forever."

It was like reaching port after a tempestuous night at sea.
Peace...God's peace that surpasses all understanding.

Difficult Beginnings

The first steps in the religious life are always difficult ones, and Theresa did not find them any easier than other people. Instead of the playful child the community had almost dreaded to admit, they discovered in the new postulant a soul that was humble, strong and generous. Her holiness she kept hidden under the appearance of simplicity.

In her first trial of humility we have seen how peaceful and serene was her attitude under the scathing comments of Monsignor Delatroette at her entry into Carmel, and he did not see fit to change his opinion of her until the year 1891, at the time of the terrible influenza epidemic which did not spare even the doors of the secluded Carmel at Lisieux. The convent was transformed into a hospital, a place of suffering and death. Numbers died each day.

It was then that Monsignor Delatroette had to change his opinion about the immaturity of Sister Theresa. When he entered the cloister to visit the sick members of the community he saw the little sister at her work. He noticed her constant sacrifices, invariably performed with a smile, and suddenly all his hostility was turned to admiration. He could scarcely speak of her after that without being moved.

Like St. Thomas he had to see in order to believe what so many others had told him.

When they reported to him that her six months as a postulant had been successful beyond all their expectations, he wished for further proof, so they lengthened the time three months. The fact that it was not made still longer was due to the influence of the mother prioress, who was firm and succeeded in having her way.

When Monsignor Delatroette was told later that Sister Theresa's novitiate had exceeded expectations, he extended that period to slightly less than two years instead of the one which is usual. In all these delays, which were disappointing to Sister Theresa's aching, longing heart, she never showed herself anything but peaceful, humble and resigned.

When she learned that the date of her profession was put off again, she exclaimed: "Oh! My dear Lord, I no longer ask to be professed. I will wait on your holy will for that, but what I could not bear would be that my union with you should be deferred through any fault of mine. So I wish to impose on myself any sacrifice in order to make a bridal garment adorned with the brilliant gems of every virtue, to make myself pleasing in your eyes and when you find my garment resplendent enough, then let nothing stand in the way of the espousal."

Instead of depressing her these trials had a stimulating effect which enabled her to redouble her zeal. They gave her renewed strength for her life of sacrifice, animated by her love. This was her way: "I suffer lovingly, and love while suffering."

During the influenza epidemic of 1891, when those more fortunate had to get up and attend the ones who were ill, Theresa, although suffering greatly with a high temperature, dedicated herself day and night to her sisters in religion, without any thought of herself. Without rest and without signs of fatigue she had words of comfort on her lips for everyone and an ever ready smile.

At the same time she also had sole charge of the sacristy, which was not light work by any means. She found the strength to perform her duties in the daily reception of Holy Communion, which was then permitted to her.

In addition to the hostility of the superior of the Order, Theresa also had to contend with the excessive harshness of the mother prioress, Mother Marie Gonzaga. Born of a noble family in Caen, she had from her early novitiate shown signs of initiative and intuition. Because of these gifts and her commanding presence, she had been elected prioress. While she was active, energetic and talented, she lacked other qualities for the office. She was impressionable and morose. She was devoid of real balance in character, and also had no sense of humor, things which all go to the making up of a good ruler. Well aware of her talents she considered herself indispensable. In fact, she thought she was the only one capable of governing the convent.

She did not like the advent in the community of so many of the Martin sisters, fearing perhaps, that they would create a nucleus or a faction against her in Carmel, where her many gifts had always been lauded and appreciated. This praise was at times a little forced, and doubtless accounted for the lack of unity existing at the time in the convent.

She had approved of Theresa Martin's entrance and welcomed her. Theresa, on her side, at first felt attracted to the mother prioress, who well knew how to charm people when she chose. The little postulant found comfort with her in the beginning when all things were looking so very dark for her. This was not for long, however, since Theresa, who had left the world without attachment to any creature, would not let herself give way to an affection she feared might grow and prevent her seeking God alone. She did violence to her feelings and denied herself the pleasure of seeing her prioress except when necessity compelled her to do so.

The mother prioress on her part, not being very spiritual minded, could not perceive any motive for this aloofness and was offended by it, so she repulsed Theresa, not in the least understanding her. She looked upon Theresa's reserved manner as a form of pride and thought her presumptuous. She feared that her youth and her sisters' companionship would turn Monsignor Delatroette's words into a prophecy. Consequently she considered it her duty to humiliate Theresa mercilessly, finding fault with everything she did. At times she took no notice of her and maintained a reserved attitude.

Theresa suffered in silence. Mother Agnes suffered even more than she did, and one day actually ventured timidly to speak of it to Mother Marie Gonzaga. Why not make allowance for her sister's youth and the great sensitivity of her nature?... "That is the result of having three sisters in one convent," was the harsh response. "No doubt you would like to see Theresa made as much of as she was at home, but I am going to do exactly the contrary, because she is much more conceited than you think," said Mother Marie Gonzaga. Mother Agnes never uttered another word. The Lord allowed the mother prioress to see pride and conceit in Theresa, so it became difficult to condemn her entirely for doing what she considered her duty, which was to make Theresa humble by humiliating her.

Theresa, who really was humble, bore with equanimity and serenity of spirit the many fault-findings and humiliations. Later, Mother Gonzaga herself had to admit in all truth, that Theresa had never failed once in perfect obedience. Later still, the prioress had to confess, "She was perfect...an angel!" and that she was astounded to find in a girl of fifteen so much prudence and soberness of judgment. "A nature of that quality does not need any soft words and tender looks," she said. "She needs an iron rule and she will follow it."

Theresa was grateful to her, for later she said: "How I thank you, dear Mother, for never having spared me. Without the regenerating work of humiliation, which vivifies, your poor little flower would not have been able to grow any roots on account of her weakness. Our Lord well knew this and to you, therefore, dear Mother, do I owe a debt of gratitude."

"My dear daughter," Mother Marie Gonzaga said to her on her deathbed, "you are on the point of appearing before God's tribunal, but you need have no fear. You have always understood and practiced humility." What a wonderful testimonial!

The humble Theresa pondered over these words and replied with all the simplicity of her heart, "Yes, I feel it; my soul only seeks the truth and I have understood humility of heart." After all, what is humility of heart, if it is not the planting of truth in the soul to recognize one's own nothingness with regard to God and one's neighbor?

We have said so much about Theresa's prioress; now let us consider her novice mistress. Theresa says of her: "She was a saintly nun, a perfect type of a Carmelite." Good, full of piety, one of a large family, and strong in faith, she was known for her sweetness and common sense, her meekness and prudence. She was very fond of Theresa and didn't hide it from her. She admired and esteemed her; she suffered for her too, and without intending it, she made Theresa suffer also.

It was quite a different suffering from that caused Theresa by Mother Marie Gonzaga. The trouble with the prioress was that one could never please her even with all the good will in the world. The novice mistress, on the other hand, did not understand Theresa in another way. She could not see that Theresa was a real contemplative, and that she had great need of silence of soul. Every day Theresa would have to listen to long exhortations, often not to the point, and these prevented her from being able to commune with God. Moreover, between the two of them, the novice mistress made things worse for Theresa with the mother prioress.

For instance, Theresa had been instructed to go and weed the garden every day at a certain time. Invariably, she would meet the mother prioress on her way who would exclaim: "What can we do with such a child who is sent for a walk in the garden every day?"

Sometimes seeing her looking poorly and tired from the austerities of the Rule, the Mistress would oblige her to rise later in the morning. Very often, however, Theresa would forget to do so, and to make up for the loss of memory she was obliged to rise later each morning for a fortnight. The mother prioress not seeing Theresa at morning meditation would scold her, and she no longer knew which one to obey. Her embarrassment was great. She was unhappy, but did not murmur. She was told that when she felt ill in any way she was to report it at once. Now Theresa always felt sick every morning, so each day she had to go and say: "I feel sick." "I would rather go up and ask for a hundred lashes instead," she said. "Poor child," is all the novice mistress would reply, having already forgotten the command she had given her, adding: "The Rule is too severe for her; she hasn't the strength or the health for it," and off she would go to report to the mother prioress. The latter, who had an excellent memory and a rather hasty temper, retorted: "This child does nothing but complain; if she can't stand the Rule she had better go; this is no place for her."

Poor Theresa had this repeated to her daily, causing her great sorrow, but as the order had not been withdrawn she continued to report each morning, "I feel sick." She lived in constant fear of having to leave the convent. Who will deny the heroism of this oft repeated act of obedience?

At last by the will of God she was liberated from this

trial. Because Theresa never showed her feelings, no one was aware of what she suffered. Her novice mistress, who was sensitive and temperamental, turned everything into a cross to be borne, and it wasn't the novice who went to the mistress for the comfort, but the mistress who sought sympathy from everyone for the little contradictions she had to endure. Talking of it later she said: "Oh, how well Theresa knew how to comfort one." Everyone who heard her could feelingly say the same, because all had received help and sympathy from her. Nevertheless, the mistress and Theresa loved each other dearly, and it was quite touching to hear this aged nun testify with all her heart to Theresa's goodness and sanctity while a novice.

She told of a night following a day of great tribulation for little Theresa, then only a postulant. The old mistress went up to her cell to see if she could comfort her and found her ready to retire. With her white gown down to her feet and her fair curls forming a halo of spun gold around her sweet face, she seemed a supernatural vision to the old Mother.

Theresa's simplicity, and her profound silence were not understood by her novice mistress, nor by Mother Genevieve, the foundress of that Carmel.

Although said to be gifted with prophetic powers, it is strange that Mother Genevieve never foresaw the future sanctity of this child. She told her to serve God with peace and joy, and to remember always that God is a God of peace. Although she did not understand Theresa, yet she was undoubtedly holy, and Sister Theresa venerated her.

On the other hand, one of the aged nuns did understand Sister Theresa's simplicity of soul. Meeting her at recreation, she said to her in passing: "Your soul is extremely simple, and when it has reached perfection it will become even more simple, because the nearer a soul advances toward God the more simple it becomes."

Sister Theresa had great difficulty in revealing her thoughts and feelings to others. She couldn't express what was going on in her soul and the spiritual conferences she had with the novice mistress were torture to her.

If only she could get comfort from heaven or help from her confessor, but heaven seemed closed to her. Besides, she suffered from aridity and sadness of soul. Everything was difficult and cost her much effort. It was only by exercising great strength of will that she could accomplish anything.

She wanted to please God in everything and to do his holy will. Now he seemed to have completely hidden himself from her and to be deaf to her prayers. She couldn't think clearly in her state, and she wondered if she was an object of love or of hate to the One she desired so ardently to serve.

Her confessor was an invalid and had to curtail his spiritual activities so she received very little help from him.

"Many a time," Mother Agnes tells us, "her confessors, not understanding her, only succeeded in alarming her and curbing her ardent zeal."

Fortunately, however, for our little saint, there came to Carmel a certain Father Pichon, S.J., who was able to restore her peace of mind and encourage her. He told her she was greatly loved, and that her interior sufferings were a proof of this. He also assured her that she had never lost her baptismal innocence, nor had she ever gravely offended her Lord. What balm, what consolation, for that poor, tormented heart!

Certainly Father Pichon restored her peace of soul, but peace of soul does not by any means put an end to difficulties and troubles, and Sister Theresa continued to suffer. Those who have a sure knowledge of being loved by God have also a complete understanding of the motives of the Beloved. She realized that all her trials were sent out of love and in return she must give to Jesus love for love.

"My child," said her confessor, "let our Lord himself ever be your Novice Master," and this she did henceforth.

Very soon after Father Pichon became her director his superiors sent him to Canada. Theresa was only able to hear from him once a year, so she promptly turned to Jesus himself. She abandoned herself entirely to his tender care, guidance and protection, permitting him to form her character. In a word, he became her life, her all.

In the school of suffering, which she understood so well, she saw that love sweetens every pain. Although ignored by her companions and subjected to many trials, which humanly speaking she could not have borne, she still lived in a state of complete serenity and peace.

"You are right, Celine," Theresa wrote her, "quite right. Life is often a bitter and a heavy burden, especially when Jesus hides himself from our love.... I wonder what this Beloved Friend is doing. Does he not see the anguish of mind we are laboring under? Where is he? Why does he not come to our aid? Celine, dear, do not fear anything. He is here, quite, quite close to us all the time. This suffering of ours, these tears, he needs them for other souls, perhaps for our own, and he wishes to reward us in his own way.

"To make us drink the bitter gall is no pleasure to him, but he knows that in this way we can become more like him. What a destiny for mere mortal man. What a grand thing a soul must be!

"Let us rise above the petty things that happen and pass. Let us keep far from this world, the air is purer higher up.... Jesus can hide himself, but the heart that loves him will always find him."

A most terrible aridity came over Theresa's spirit during her holy retreats before the ceremonies of her investiture, or clothing, and of her profession.

Before the former she wrote to Mother Agnes that she

was content to suffer greatly and that what she most desired was to be able to forget entirely the things of this world.

Why should she care about any worldly things? She felt her soul was too big to be contented with any of them, but how small her soul seemed when she compared it with the Infinite Jesus.

She thought that if God were to send her even a tiny grain of happiness, she might become attached to it with all her heart, but this was denied her. In this she could trace the great goodness and love of God, who will not permit one of his cherished ones to become attached to any creature. "I do not wish any creature to have any part of my love," she said. "I want it all for Jesus. He has given me to understand that in him only is to be found real and lasting happiness. Everything must be for him, everything! And when, like this evening, I have nothing to offer him, well, I must give him that, 'nothing.'"

It is always by way of the cross that one reaches sanctity, just as Theresa did. She suffered much, but it was hidden in her soul. It was known only to God, but concealed from the eyes of human beings.

The day of her investiture was a joy and a triumph, but that of her profession was bathed in tears. The night before, when she was watching before the Blessed Sacrament, the devil made a terrible assault on her. All of a sudden a feeling came over her that the Carmelite life for her was a delusion, that she was not meant for it and could not persevere in it. She was in complete darkness and really thought that she should return to the world. She revealed this temptation to the Reverend Mother, who couldn't help laughing. Immediately the devil fled and the temptation left her.

As the community wended its way to the chapter room a flight of swallows circled the convent. Was it an image of Theresa's eager flight to meet her Bridegroom? All nature was joyful and smiling. Theresa's soul was flooded with peace, but not with joy. It was an enveloping peace of soul, and in that spirit she pronounced her vows. This was on September 8, 1890. The actual taking of the veil was fixed for September 24, when the family would be allowed to be present.

Theresa hoped that her father would be able to come, but that was not to be.

Another disappointment was the absence of Bishop Hugonin, who had promised to conduct the ceremony.

Theresa cried at not being able to have her father present. These tears caused uncharitable comment, and once more she was misunderstood. Yet, were not her tears very natural? She owed her dear father so much and loved him dearly.

Poor little Theresa!

Her sister Marie, seeing her decorating the statue of the Infant Jesus in the cloister (which was one of her duties) with little remnants of candle ends, asked her why she didn't use the pretty pink ones which her father had given her for her investiture day. Theresa replied that at the investiture her father had been present and all had to be beautiful, but that now they seemed quite inappropriate.

For her there would henceforth be only heavenly joys and pleasures to look forward to, in that paradise where all created things give way to uncreated reality.

In the second great retreat before her profession, Theresa, to reveal her dispositions, gives us a similitude. She desired, she said, to reach the summit of the mountain of love. By which road and what means would it be possible? She left that to God. He would take her by the hand and lead her through a dark tunnel, where the only light would be that of the Holy Face of Jesus. Jesus would be silent and Theresa would be silent too, but she would tell him that she loved him more than anything else.

She was advancing toward her goal, she could not say

how, because she was all in darkness, but something in her heart told her that she was approaching the crest of the mountain.

She walked in impenetrable darkness and she thanked God for it. She was content that the darkness should surround her all her life, if, by this, she could bring light to sinners. Her real happiness consisted in not having any consolations.

She would have been ashamed to be like the promised brides of the world who have their eyes on the hands of the bridegroom, seeking for gifts or searching his face for a smile that would be proof of his love.

Theresa did not love Jesus for his gifts or his smiles, but for himself alone. She was attracted by his hidden tears. To discover them she kept her eyes fixed on him so as to gather them as precious diamonds.

After giving us this similitude, which reveals the purity of her love, she discarded interest in all things, even the spiritual.

"Jesus, I want to love you so much! I want to love you as you have never been loved before! At any cost to myself I crave the palm of martyrdom. If it cannot be of blood, let it be a martyrdom of love."

These words reveal to us the depth of her sanctity and the why and wherefore of her glory. These are the thoughts and aspirations that were considered audacious by human creatures, but were eminently blessed by heaven.

As we have seen, the day of Theresa's investiture was a feast of light and joy, a real triumph. Quite contrary to custom, at the end of the ceremony the bishop intoned the "Te Deum." The master of ceremonies endeavored to stop him, but it was at once taken up enthusiastically by all and continued. That "Te Deum" was an echo of joy from heaven. In fact, thirty-six years later, under the dome of St. Peter's in Rome, Pius XI intoned the "Te Deum" which again was sung by thousands of people, their eyes fixed on a large painting surrounded by a blaze of light; a picture of the humble little Saint Theresa of the Child Jesus and the Holy Face, in her glory. St. Theresa pray for us!

The day of her investiture in Lisieux, January 10, 1889, was a very mild day, but it snowed during the ceremony in gratification of a longing of Theresa's to see the earth decked in spotless white. Was this a symbol of her purity?

Where, she said, could one find an earthly lover, however powerful, capable of making one snowflake fall to please his beloved? Thirty-six years later, on the day of her canonization, airplanes circled over the Square of St. Peter's showering petals of roses.

She promised to send down a "shower of roses," by which she meant graces and blessings. Certainly her heavenly Bridegroom has on numerous occasions gratified this desire. She has many grateful clients who bless her name and her sanctity.

All her life she had one aim, and one only, that of pleasing Jesus. Now Jesus seems to like to reciprocate by pleasing her.

Theresa's life was only a short one, but as long as time lasts she will continue to receive "roses" from his sacred hands to shower them upon those on earth who invoke her help.

On May 17, 1925, St. Peter's Basilica was a blaze of light, a figure of the resplendence of the saintly soul of Theresa and the celebrating of a new feast of the Church. This brings to our mind the words of the Gospel about the little child in the midst of the disciples whom our Lord held up as an example to them. "Unless you become as a little child, you cannot enter into the kingdom of heaven."

In the Shadow of the Cloister

The life in a Carmelite convent is not difficult to describe, one day being very much like another.

It is an apostolate where victories are hidden and known only to God. Theresa had a very lofty and beautiful mission to fulfill, but her efforts were not crowned until after her death. Everything in her life denoted simplicity. She told us of her daily occupations from the time she entered Carmel.

"When I first entered the convent," she said, "I was put in charge of the linen cupboard as assistant to the mother sub-prioress (Sister Marie of the Angels). I also had to sweep the stairs and one of the dormitories. Then I had to go and weed the garden—a thing that invariably annoyed the mother prioress.

"From the day of my clothing until I was eighteen, I swept the refectory and filled the water decanters.

"For the 'Forty Hours' in 1891, I was placed in charge of the sacristy, and from June of the following year I didn't have any special work allotted me. It was then that I had time to paint the fresco around the tabernacle of the oratory. I was also third purser."

In this account of her various duties which she narrated with touching simplicity, she entirely omitted a very important one confided to her care. There was no glory attached to it. Her life was to be hidden, unknown.

She was made assistant to the novice mistress, and shortly after, mistress of novices, but in her humility she begged to be called, instead, "Elder Sister of the Novices." This office was confided to her under delicate and difficult circumstances and she thought it was really beyond her ability. It had been imposed on her under the command of obedience, and she could not refuse.

Sister Theresa, who was always humble and simple, ran to hide herself in God's embrace. She explained to him how helpless she was, and that she didn't feel able to nurture his children. She would like to make a bargain with him— she would put out her hand toward him, and he, in turn, would place into it sufficient grace for each soul.

Finding the direction helpful, the novices would know that it didn't come from her but from God. If they found the direction bitter, they would likewise know that it came from God and hold her blameless, and thus could she keep her peace of soul.

For herself, she only desired one thing, and that was to find the means for attaching herself closer and closer to God, knowing full well that all would be added to her.

As soon as she assumed this duty with the novices, she implored God not to let her evoke any affection in others, and this was granted to her. She was loved, it is true, for her sterling qualities, and her exemplary life.

She never disguised the truth, however unpalatable it might be. "It behooves one," she said, "to be absolutely truthful in dealing with souls confided to our care. If they do not actually love me for my candor, it does not matter; it is not their good opinion that I seek."

Studying and examining other people's conduct was extremely distasteful to her. In order to be of help to the novices, she had to observe their slightest faults and defects, so that they might overcome them.

But in view of her pact with Jesus, she found she could watch them impersonally as from a high tower. Nothing escaped her, not one of the Evil One's maneuvers was unknown to her. She was quite surprised at herself.

Nevertheless, she found this task immensely distasteful. She realized that this should be so, for if it were pleasant to her to reprove, resentment might be the motive that inspired the correction.

Sometimes, though, it was a question of having to control a rebellious nature, but she must not be discouraged. Jesus had given her the grace of not fearing her duty, and she would not shirk it at any cost.

Theresa was quite fearless at times. She would risk the censure of the novice mistress when she found it necessary to admonish and help the novices to overcome their imperfections.

Celine, who, by then had become Sister Genevieve of the Holy Face, was one of Sister Theresa's novices and inclined to think her quite severe toward them, but "not enough to call it a defect. Her admonitions were ever holy ones and directed mostly toward those who hadn't proper command over themselves and their senses. She was always very calm when reprimanding, quite as much as if she were recollected in prayer. Even on her deathbed she continued to fight against her own imperfections and those of her sisters, the novices."

Mother Agnes smilingly said: "Here lies our warrior beaten down!"

"Not at all," replied Sister Theresa, "because I have never used other weapons than the sword of the spirit, that is, the word of God. Therefore, illness cannot overcome me. Only yesterday evening did I use my spiritual sword against one of the novices. As I have often said before, I shall die with my sword in my hand."

She was irreproachable in regularity and in the observance of the Rule, and she saw to it that her novices were the same. They, one and all, could testify that they had never seen her break the smallest Rule.

Whenever the reverend mother prioress informed them that she wished something done, Theresa carried out the order to the letter.

At the sound of the bell she would instantly lay down whatever she was doing. She would interrupt a sentence, no matter how interesting the conversation, leave her needle in her sewing without even pulling it through and lay aside the work at once. All her life she showed a heroic obedience.

Once when stricken with fever, Marie, to ease her somewhat, was about to remove the great heavy blanket from the bed, but Sister Theresa restrained her. "It would be a relief," she said, "but I don't know if it is permitted. I would rather retain it until you can get permission from the reverend mother." In fact she kept this heavy cover on to the end, in spite of the terrible discomfort it caused her because she had once heard Mother Marie Gonzaga say to a strong, robust, young nun that it was a laudable act of mortification to keep a blanket on sometimes in the heat of the summer.

"No matter how many people break the Rule," she would say, "that is no reason why I should feel justified in doing so. Everyone should act as if the whole perfection of the Order rested personally on her shoulders." She was very severe concerning touchiness, laziness, doing things so as to attract attention, or making a fuss over any little complaint or suffering. She wished her novices to be strong in character, not gossiping or manifesting self-pity. They were to be self-sufficient and able to perform their own duties to the very best of their ability, without seeking help from others.

She had always managed without asking for any favors or privileges, and they were to do likewise. If they felt inclined to ask for a dispensation of any kind, they should ask themselves this question, "What if everyone did the same?"

"The reply you will give yourself will very soon show you what a state of disorder would follow and how important it is to keep a proper balance in all things."

Generous and energetic, she never refused to self what she expected from others, and in all things gave them a wonderful example of virtue and sanctity. Meeting a young novice moving slowly out of the laundry room she asked: "Is it thus you would move if you had a large family to feed?"

She was firm, but oh! so good to everyone, always. St. Mary Magdalene de Pazzi called her novices her little doves. Sister Theresa named hers her little lambs. She had for them the heart of a mother. She did everything to spur them on, and to encourage them. Even her rebukes came from her great motherly love.

This is how she describes her difficult, and often thankless task: "Running after little lambs, pointing out to them that they have soiled their white fleece, and confronting them with a small particle of their wool left clinging to the weeds and tares of life."

Her counsels and her little notes to them are enchanting in their wisdom, goodness and tenderest simplicity. We would never gather from any of them the severity that Celine mentioned.

Monsignor Laveille said, "She used a powerful lever in urging them [the novices] to do their best. It was the thought of Jesus' great love for us and his infinite mercy.

"With this constant thought of our Divine Redeemer before her eyes, she would arouse flagging spirits, instill courage where it was lacking and give the taste for perfection and the hope of acquiring it."

About a year after her profession she suffered a great

loss in the person of Mother Genevieve of St. Theresa, whom everyone looked upon as a saint and from whom on the day of her death, Sister Theresa received a most particular grace.

It was the first time she had been present at a death, and she found it beautiful, although her heart was steeped in sorrow. All of a sudden, her soul was flooded with a supernatural joy, and she presumed that at that moment the soul of the dear Mother was entering heaven. She felt sure the saintly Mother was letting her share a little of her celestial happiness.

Theresa further relates of her that some time before she died she questioned Mother Genevieve, "Oh! Mother, you will surely never go to purgatory!" "I hope not," Mother Genevieve answered with simplicity.

"Certain it is," said St. Theresa, "that God would not disappoint one who had hoped with such humility, and now the graces we have received through her intercession are a proof of it."

Every one of the sisters endeavored to obtain a relic of her. Theresa also wished very much to possess one, and secured hers almost immediately after the saintly nun's death, in this manner: She had noticed a tear in her eye which had been forced from her in her last agony. Taking a small piece of fine linen Theresa secured this priceless treasure and showed it to Reverend Mother Prioress, who permitted her to keep it.

The Little Way

Theresa was simple in all her ways with others, and equally simple in the intimacy of her own soul.

In heaven she may well serve as a beacon of light to those who are still traveling in darkness and who will be glad to follow her example, especially since in her outward appearances there didn't seem to be anything heroic, magnanimous or spectacular about her way of life.

God sent her into the world to be a guide to weak and timorous souls, souls, perhaps, with high and noble aspirations but weak in will, to whom the hill of sanctity seems practically insurmountable; especially in comparison with the lives of the austere saints of ancient times.

To those who hesitate and are discouraged at the foot of the mount, not daring to move one way or the other, Theresa has shown a little path, an easy way. She, herself, will take them by the hand; will teach them her secret; will reveal her asceticism in all its littleness, and will make them strong and generous.

Better still, she will adopt them and manifest to them her "little way." Being so small then, she will place them in the arms of Jesus to repose on his Heart.

Can these people compete with the great saints, the anchorites, the martyrs, the confessors? Yes. Perhaps they will even surpass them, but quite simply and without knowing or even imagining it. It was thus for Theresa. From the martyrs, the hermits, the doctors, the founders of religious Orders, the reformers, and all the saints devoted to the Sacred Heart we have gradually arrived at this new mode of sanctity, a form no less beautiful, but just as real, and accessible to all. God has presented to his creatures a form of sanctity in harmony with the times; and now that we are living in an age of his great mercy, it would seem as though he offers us his Sacred Heart and says to each one: "I desire you all to be saints."

This generation is full of pride. Theresa, with her particular form of sanctity, so loving and so childlike, has given us the antidote.

The world is full of feverish activity. Theresa has shown us that sanctity does not depend on a multiplicity of actions performed in a sublime manner, but rather in the amount of love we put into them, a love that gives life to each little thing and at the same time so purifies each action that it becomes worthy to rise like incense to the very throne of God.

Our effete century dreads any austerity. Here, again, Theresa showed us that sanctity is not necessarily based on making our body suffer great pain, but that it is a habitual state of soul, a continual sacrifice of mind, heart and will. Therefore, the body suffers but in a different way.

Theresa did not practice penance for penance's sake, or suffer pain for the sake of suffering. She did all and suffered everything lovingly for God.

Hence Theresa pointed out her "little way." To make it a real help to us, God let her endure all the weaknesses of human nature, and helped her to triumph over them. In fact, she was handicapped by a very shy and sensitive nature, and was easily given to tears.

She suffered a martyrdom of scruples, she felt a great need of friendship, and she liked praise and approbation.

She was tempted for a moment to discontinue the efforts toward perfection she was making. She had strong likes and dislikes for the people with whom she lived, a common occurrence when people of different temperaments live together. At one time she was sorely tempted against faith, but nothing succeeded in turning her from her love. She bore all these trials with simplicity and great patience of soul, and overcame them.

While convinced of her weakness and helplessness, nevertheless she had great aspirations towards sanctity from her childhood.

Comparing herself with the great saints, she saw them rising as giant mountains whose crests are lost in the clouds and herself as a little grain of sand at the foot of one of them. She did not lose courage, however. She would be the little grain of sand trodden under foot by the passer-by. God would not have put such a strong desire in her heart to be a saint, if she were not capable of attaining it. Notwithstanding all her imperfections, she determined to strive to climb the hill of sanctity.

Could she, of herself, perform this stupendous task? No.

At first she tried her body, as so many saints have done. She wore a little iron cross with sharp points that dug into her soft flesh with every movement she made. Because this caused a bad wound, she was forbidden to wear the cross any longer.

She no longer dared to practice the severe austerities of the mystic as she felt she was too small. What then could she do?

She would conquer herself, with all her weaknesses and faults. She would try to be little, for is not being as a little child the first step towards sanctity? Jesus gave the little child as a model to his disciples, and told Nicodemus to be born again, though he was a noted doctor in Israel.

Well, then, Theresa would remain as a child. She must find a simple and easy way to reach heaven.

She would choose something new, living in an age of modern inventions...the elevator, for instance, which carries one up without any inconvenience.... She must find a spiritual "elevator" to carry her up the steep way of perfection.

She searched for it in Sacred Scripture. Opening to Proverbs, she found: "If anyone is very small let him come to me." So she approached God, because no one can be smaller than she. What would God do with this little one? She found that Isaiah said: "As a mother fondles her child, so will I console you. I will carry you in my arms and will sit you on my knee." So she found her "elevator" in the arms of Jesus!

No more simple way of climbing the steps of perfection could she have found, and all she had to do was to remain as a little child, so that she could always be carried in the arms of Jesus, instead of climbing by her own efforts. To remain so insignificantly small she had first of all to realize her utter nothingness, expecting all from God, just as a child does with regard to its father, having no anxiety for the future. So without giving herself any credit for any good she did, she did not become discouraged over her many faults. Infants often fall yet do not hurt themselves much in so doing. The child as he grows tries to be more independent. He struggles in his mother's arms, wishing to be free to take his first steps, and finds his mother's restraining arm an obstacle. Others are content to repose peacefully, letting her judge for them.

Theresa preferred to be like the latter. She shut her mind to all vain arguments to make useless quests or personal efforts. She placidly fell asleep in Jesus' arms, feeling perfectly safe and at peace.

She let him carry her where he would. He thought for

her, loved for her, spoke for her, acted for her. All her actions were subjected to his will.

Those who thus abandon themselves, believing, hoping and living in this manner, are persons of strong and powerful love. And after all, what does God ask of his creatures other than love? He tells us that he does not need our words, only our love.

This service of love and thanksgiving is precisely what Theresa rendered to him throughout her whole life—forgetting, conquering, and sacrificing herself.

"How easy it is, O Lord, to love you," she exclaimed, and by her example she taught us this strong and tender love, always confident and childlike, the source in her of so many other perfections. She had obtained the grace of this love in return for a very rare virtue which blossomed in her childhood, that of her voluntary, complete, and daily cooperation with the divine will.

The Strong Lever

Love is the strongest motivating power we know in life, and Theresa knew how to use this potent lever from early childhood.

When she entered Carmel she would have thrown herself into the sea of love without any fear and in full confidence, but her elders thought her too venturesome and full of zeal for one so young. It wasn't until a holy Franciscan, Father Alexis, came to the convent that she was able to float her barque on that sea with sail full set, looking only ahead, in spite of the many tribulations she had had to endure at the time of her profession.

Father Alexis was a good missionary, more adapted to catching sinners than to helping saints. Theresa facetiously said: "I must be a great sinner, therefore, because he at once understood me and encouraged me." In fact he spurred her on to even greater efforts and he was able to assure her that Jesus was well pleased with her, and that she had never really offended him with her imperfections.

It was the first time she had been told of imperfections not offending God, but she had felt convinced of this fact for a long time.

The heart of God is even more tender than that of a mother. Now, a mother is always ready to forgive the petty faults of her little child, and Theresa remembered how contrite she always felt when Pauline caressed her instead of chiding her as she expected.

Her nature was such that fear always restrained her, but with love she was capable of great things. She didn't merely rise, she soared.

God, who said he has no need of creatures, nevertheless stooped to beg a little water from the Samaritan woman in these words: "Give me to drink." Under these words he concealed his thirst for love. Alas! that there are so many hard-hearted people in the world, so many ingrates!

In 1895 Theresa pondered the courage of so many generous people who offered themselves as victims of divine justice, drawing down on themselves the punishment due to sinners. She admired them with all her heart but she could not emulate them. However, another thought preoccupied her. Was only the divine justice to receive victims offered in holocaust? What about that great, merciful love, so misunderstood, neglected and despised? The Heart of Jesus is a furnace from which springs eternal flames. Instead of running to be inflamed with its burning heat, giving him love for love, his creatures turn their backs on him and seek fleeting pleasures in the world.

Is all this despised love to remain shut up in the heart of God? If he were to find some people ready to welcome him, who would offer themselves to him in holocaust just for love, would he not utterly consume them with the fire of this love, and be happy no longer to have to repress it but to give of it freely in return?

On June 9, 1895, with the permission of the Reverend Mother Prioress, Theresa offered herself to God as a victim of love. From that moment she found herself, as it were, immersed in a sea of wonderful graces. She felt herself surrounded and inflamed with love. She had reached the height of her desire.

It no longer sufficed for her to be a Carmelite and mother of souls. She felt a vocation to be a warrior, priest, apostle, doctor, martyr!

She wanted to perform the most heroic actions, such as going on the crusades, or dying on the field of battle for the defense of the Church.

She longed to be a priest, at the same time admiring the humility of St. Francis, who refused the sublime honor of being one.

What wouldn't she have given to go all over the world preaching the Gospel! To plant the cross in unchristian countries and receive in one embrace all the missions and missionaries who had evangelized the world since its creation.

She wished for martyrdom, not for one kind, but all of them, beginning with the flagellation and crucifixion of her divine Savior.

She would have loved to emulate for God all the actions of the saints described in books that she had read.

It was more than a thirst, it was a raging fire that consumed her.

She searched the Epistles of St. Paul and found that it is impossible to be at the same time an apostle, a prophet, and a doctor.

The Church is composed of various members and each one has his particular part to fulfill. For instance, an eye cannot be a hand, as the function of each is different.

This she found quite clear as far as it went, but she read further.

The Apostle recommended one to ardently seek after high virtues, but even these, he said, are as nothing without love, and he explained that charity is the surest way of reaching God.

Considering the Mystical Body of Christ, which is the Church, Theresa did not perceive in herself any of these members described by St. Paul, but she desired to be all of them.

Charity, though, was what gave her the real key to her vocation.

If the Church has a body, it must also have a heart, and this heart must burn with charity!

Moreover, if this heart ceased to beat, the members could not survive and there would be no more apostles to preach the Gospel, nor martyrs to shed their blood.

All vocations are born of love. Love embraces all; it is eternal and in every place in all ages, never ending.

This was, indeed, Theresa's great discovery. She had found her real vocation at last. In the heart of the Church she would be love, and being love she would be all, and therefore her dream would be realized.

Sister Theresa felt she was so small, just like a little fledgling in the nest, a wee bird covered with only a few feathers, still unable to fly.

It was wonderful to see her conscious of her weakness and defects, but full of these daring thoughts and seemingly with little power to accomplish any of her desires. They were realized, however, by many saints who are in heaven, each one who followed a vocation along the lines to which Theresa aspired.

She appealed to these dear saints and humbly asked them to adopt her as a daughter.

While God's priests were doing battle in the field to win souls for Christ, she would stand by the throne of God, loving and praying for those who were fighting. In order to show her love, she scattered spiritual flowers before the throne of God; she sang the canticle of love with her silver toned voice.

Here, then, is the "little way" pointed out by St. Theresa to all timid and weak souls, to rest quietly and confidently in God's loving arms, to be ever a child, and to love ardently and generously.

"Oh! if only weak and imperfect souls like mine," she said, "could feel what I feel, not one would ever despair of reaching the summit of the mountain of love, because Jesus does not ask for great works but only for our hearts, our confidences, and our gratitude."

Scattering Flowers

To scatter flowers! With this poetical description Theresa throws a veil of simplicity over a whole life spent in sacrifice.

The total immolation of self and her scattering of flowers was for her a daily collection of sacrifices, never letting any opportunity escape her, even a glance or a word. She must curb them all, just for love; to suffer with love, to enjoy with love, and to offer all the flowers of her sacrifices to Jesus; to scatter them before him, singing all the while, even though they have to be gathered from among the thorns. In fact, the longer the thorns, the sweeter must be her song. Let us consider a few of these flowers scattered by Theresa on her way, and we shall be better able to understand the number of them and the scope of her life.

One of the sisters of Carmel had the faculty of annoying Theresa greatly in many ways. One day this sister meeting her in the corridor stopped her and asked: "Can you tell me, Sr. Theresa, why you are so greatly attracted to me? I never meet you that you don't give me a charming smile."

Poor Sister, if she only knew! But Jesus was the only one who knew what Theresa had hidden in her heart; Jesus, who can always sweeten what is bitter, and to whom she flew in all her troubles.

To be able to dominate and to conquer self she must go beyond the unattractive attributes of her neighbor and seek the help of him who dwells in the soul which is in a state of grace.

She was so friendly with that sister, and her victory over self was so complete, that Sister Marie of the Sacred Heart was not a little jealous of her and complained jokingly to Theresa: "I think you love Sister X better than you do me! When you meet her you smile your sweetest and we, your own sisters, don't get treated half so well. It seems to me one's own flesh and blood ought to come first. After all, they have been given to you by God." Theresa couldn't help laughing heartily over this, but she never revealed her terrible dislike of the favored one.

To help Celine conquer her antipathies, when she was one of her novices, Theresa taught her from some of her own experiences in similar cases. On learning the name of the sister who was the cause of Theresa's antipathy, Celine was astounded. She had always thought Theresa had a special predilection for her.

Some people may go so far as to say: "Oh! I don't think much of that. Most people have their antipathies and we must all hide them, or we would soon find life very unpleasant." Granted, but can most people disguise their feelings as well in order to convince the other person that they have nothing but the kindest feelings toward them? Such conduct is high sanctity.

It must be taken into consideration, also, that they were living in a convent, confined in a small cloister, rubbing shoulders every day almost at every hour, and there was no possibility of getting away even for a time. It had to be borne, and Theresa did it with good grace.

Theresa was later told to assist a very aged nun in her various tasks, one who was particularly fitted for trying people's patience to the limit. She was desperately slow and dreadfully punctilious. Such and such a thing must be put in a certain place and turned in a certain way. Such a door must be opened or shut in a particular way. To sit down, one must go through some ceremony desired by her, etc.

The contrast between the two was ludicrous. Theresa never let the old nun see what an effort she had to make so as not to lose patience with her. She never varied in her calm serenity. Let us endeavor to imitate her.

In the last days of Theresa's life the aged sister would say with tears in her eyes: "Oh! what an angel, anyone could see she was an angel." So far so good, but then she would add: "I can aver that while she was with me I always contributed to her happiness," and this was said with such a confident smile that no one would have dared to contradict her.

What a delusion for the old nun to be under, but then what a saint the other must have been to create such an illusion!

While Sister Theresa was arranging some flowers around the coffin of Sister Genevieve, one of the lay sisters audibly remarked to another: "Look how she gives prominence to the flowers sent in by her family and hides the others underneath." Theresa, who had no other thought than the arranging of the flowers themselves to make them look their best, regardless of where they came from, turned at once to the lay sister with a smile: "You are quite right, Sister. I thank you for the hint," adding: "Would you kindly hand me the box of moss sent by the workmen?" Dismantling her whole work she rearranged the flowers according to the lay sister's suggestion. They didn't look nearly as nice, but the spiritual flowers of charity and humility were Theresa's to offer to Jesus.

What wonderful mastery of self is revealed in this little event. Thus she gathered all her flowers to be able to scatter them at the feet of her Lord. She never passed one without plucking it. What vigilance on her part never to miss one! But love, deep and true, is love ever vigilant!

There was another aged lay sister in the convent, good in her way, but partially paralyzed. She had grown stubborn and fretful in her ways. As she moved very, very slowly, dragging her feet one after the other, someone had to interrupt her devotions to assist her, and leave the chapel at ten minutes to six in order to get to the refectory in time for supper.

Jesus suggested to Theresa that she should offer herself for this thankless task, the thought of which pleased her not at all, but she offered to perform it because from the age of three she had never denied Jesus anything. She didn't find it easy to be accepted for the post. As a rule, aged people never like trusting themselves to very young ones, but Theresa managed to overcome all the old nun's objections.

When Theresa saw the invalid shake the hourglass, which told her the time, she knew it was time to move. She would then rise and taking her courage in both hands would begin some of the complicated ceremonies necessary before leaving the chapel.

First, the bench had to be moved, but woe betide if it wasn't done in the right way! Then the invalid had to be held up by her waist band from behind but not too strongly...only just so...then she can't walk too fast...but going too slow is equally tiring. Sometimes she would miss a step and would say: "That is because you were hurrying me...you are pulling me now...go slower." If Theresa held her lightly, she would complain: "You give me no support; I can't feel you at all. I must be able to feel your hand or I shall fall...I always said you were too young to be of any use to me!"

One evening, in summer, when all the air was still and

the lightest sound was carried on the air, she heard a distant orchestra playing. She pictured a large sumptuously furnished room with many lights and gold tapestries, a well-dressed crowd of young people enjoying themselves. She lowered her eyes to the brick pavement of the old cloister. What a contrast! She, helping a poor, infirm old nun, her only orchestra being the groans and sighs of the invalid as she laboriously made her way. This contrast pervaded her soul with infinite sweetness. She understood that the light of Truth was far above any poor illuminations of this world, and for centuries of pleasures such as might be enjoyed in that distant hall, she would not renounce one minute of the time given by her to this little act of charity.

On arrival at the refectory there were more petty troubles for Theresa with her charge before she was at liberty to go to her own meal. She noticed that the poor sister had great difficulty in cutting her bread, so she waited to do this also. The sister was moved to tears. No one had ever done so much for her before, and without having been asked either. Theresa never left her charge without bestowing on her her angelic smile, and she performed this good work for years.

On one occasion Theresa's serge scapular had become unfastened, and one of the sisters, noticing it, offered to pin it for her. This she did with a large safety pin, which she dug into the scapular, the habit, and Theresa's flesh! Most of us would have screamed, or made some cry of pain...but though she felt the pain, Theresa gave no sign, as she had such good control of all her senses.

Happy in the thought that no one had noticed anything, she went to the cellar, filled the wine decanters and took them upstairs and placed them on the long tables, and for many hours endured the pain that had been inflicted, until it occurred to her that she ought not to continue to do so without permission from the Mother Prioress.

In the refectory she was seated next to another old nun who had an illness which made her suffer terribly from thirst. She was supposed to share a bottle of wine with Theresa, but on many an occasion she would, out of sheer thoughtlessness, finish the bottle before Theresa had had any. Theresa, afraid that if she drank water the sister would at once perceive her mistake and be embarrassed, would go without any drink at all and say nothing.

In the laundry Theresa's tub was in front of a sister who washed all the handkerchiefs, and washing them vigorously, she would splash the dirty water in Theresa's face. Her first inclination was to do what we would all do...step backwards and wipe her face, with an expression of disgust...but not so Theresa. She at once saw in this an opportunity for collecting further jewels for her heavenly crown. Because her fastidiousness rose in revolt at the very thought of the dirty suds, she deliberately chose that very place each time, and smiled because the sacrifice was so very dear to her.

Even the cooks in the kitchen were aware of her mortifications and took advantage of them. Thus it often occurred that some leftovers would be reheated and served to Theresa for days: they knew she would never complain.

This went on for seven years until one of the sisters, more observant than the others, reported it to the Reverend Mother, saying: "That is why Theresa is always in such poor health." But Theresa, herself, never made any complaint. She had a virtue, described by the saintly foundress of the Visitation convent at Paray-le-Monial, as the "virginity of suffering."

"Everything must be for Jesus and preserved for him with jealous care," Theresa said. "It is so good to work for him alone. One's heart dilates with joy and one feels lighthearted."

She preferred going through life utterly unnoticed, like

a little grain of sand trodden underfoot, unseen and forgotten. This was her earnest desire. She would rather be
ignored than despised, because what is despised, is something, whereas what is nothing is not even thought about.

She was allotted one of the worst cells in the convent. It
was far from all the others and, besides, was bitterly cold
in winter and extremely hot in summer. In winter, after
Matins and before retiring in the evening, she went with
the others to the community room to get warm by the
stove. The sisters, when they were thoroughly warm,
would go to their cells to get to bed before the effects of
the fire would wear off.

But poor little Theresa had fifty or sixty yards of open
cloister to cross before reaching her destination. Her cell
was on the floor above, and she had many stairs to climb
and long corridors to walk. On bad days because of the
wind and rain, and sometimes the snow in the cloister, she
would be nearly frozen. In spite of the two coarse blankets
allowed on the bed, she shivered and her teeth chattered
all night. If she did doze off from sheer exhaustion, the
trembling of her limbs would waken her again. This she
endured from the age of sixteen to twenty-four, when she
died.

Her insomnia became chronic. It is difficult enough to
endure this when one is warm and comfortable in bed, but
accompanied by intense cold it becomes a terrible suffering.

Just a word to the novice mistress would have put an
end to this suffering, but she preferred to offer it to Jesus
silently. She thought she might be refusing a means of
suffering which might be very pleasing to our Lord and
give her fresh "flowers" to scatter at his feet. Besides,
wasn't this cross sent to her by him?

Only on her deathbed did she reveal these things, and
acknowledge that of all the sufferings she had undergone
at Carmel that of being so cold had been the worst.

How was her conduct in choir? In this particular convent the places in choir were allotted by the mother prioress and were permanent. Theresa, who was extremely sensitive, happened to be placed next to a sister who was never still a minute. She clicked her teeth together, twitched at her habit or scapular, coughed and cleared her throat, and the movements of her body were incessant.

For recollected prayer, silence and quiet are imperative. Therefore, these continual little noises not only distracted Theresa, but disturbed her. Her natural feelings would have led her to turn around and politely request the sister to do her best to be more quiet. Theresa, on the contrary, would not give herself this satisfaction even though the effort she made in curbing her natural impulses would cause a profuse sweat.

Her prayer must be one of endurance. She could do nothing to prevent the annoyance, but found some means of helping herself to bear it. She made up her mind to suffer it gladly. Then she learned to love it, and called it her heavenly concert, whose music must have been pleasing to Jesus, as she daily offered it to him. There is no doubt that it must have pleased Jesus greatly, since this mortification must have been all the more terrible to her because it was apparently a trivial thing, utterly unnoticed by anyone else and probably by most would have been called ridiculous.

During a retreat given by Father Alexis, which she called a "retreat of grace," her soul soared on the wings of love and complete trust.

Now, Mother Gonzaga by a capricious abuse of authority, forbade her to speak again to Father Alexis during the retreat. Just those few words she had with him at the beginning but never again! Theresa was unhappy about it, but never murmured. She was acting sacristan at the time and she could hear the priest walking up and down in the sacristy. No one went near him and she, who desired so much to speak to him, was forbidden to do so. This fact is revealed to us by the novice mistress who was very unhappy over the harshness of the mother prioress to Theresa. She was so edified at Theresa's calm generosity toward her superior that she remembered it to the end of her long life.

Someone noticed that when Theresa was very ill, she never chased away the flies that irritated and tormented her. When questioned about it, she replied: "Our Lord has commanded us to love our enemies. Now, I have no other enemies than these, so I try to bear with them and even love them."

This was another "little thing" but perhaps not thought of by others. People who consider themselves on the road to perfection will think nothing of killing an importunate fly with a gesture of resentment. It is just one more virtuous trait shown by St. Theresa, of whose heroism there can be no doubt. It not only commands our profoundest respect, but the thought of her youth makes the deepest appeal to our heart.

The episode with the flies is mentioned in "Last Words," and states that it was at the end of August—not only the hottest time of the year but also so shortly before her death (she died in September) that one can say she was also at the end of her moral and physical martyrdom.

Every evening one of the sisters came into the invalid's room and would stand at the foot of the bed and smile at her. Theresa, with an effort, would smile back, and Mother Agnes asked her if this wasn't an exertion. "Yes," she replied, "it is very inconsistent for someone in perfect health to stand and smile at you when you are in great pain, but I think of our Lord on the cross. He was in agony, and the Gospel says that many came and gazed at him, shaking their heads. It is this thought that gives me courage to offer this little sacrifice to God."

We could go on indefinitely citing edifying examples of Sister Theresa's virtue. Everything in her life revealed her constant mortification, carried on always with a smiling face. Her serene dignity, her mastery over self, were things far beyond her years.

She was ready and alert at the least signal from anyone, and willing immediately to perform any task that was required of her. To Jesus, to whom she had given all her love and whom she saw in every fresh sacrifice that presented itself, she opened her arms and her heart saying: "Come, I will give you whatever you ask of me." We know that these were no idle words on her part. She gave her all cheerfully and smilingly, for more than half her immolations were known only to Jesus. Before we criticize this little saint and say that she did nothing very wonderful, let us try imitating her. Let us try to walk in her "little way," doing all the "little" things she did, without ever letting anyone see what it costs us. Let us continue this for years, daily and unnoticed, and we will very soon find out if there was anything heroic in her mode of life. God would not have glorified her as much as he did if her path had been an easy one. All her actions proclaim her sanctity.

When one is in robust health and enjoying a tranquil mind, devotion and fervor come easily to the spiritually minded. Mortification, though never easy, is less hard to bear and can become more or less a habit. But Theresa was always delicate and ailing; she had been so from childhood. She suffered a great deal internally. We have already spoken of her insomnia. She lacked the proper sustaining food for one whose constitution required a nourishing diet. She was always parched with thirst, but never quenched it.

Her spiritual trials were numerous. Heaven seemed closed to her. She received no comfort from there and certainly none on earth. No one can deny these facts, even if they wished to do so.

How could God refuse, then, to stoop to her aid, she who never asked anything for herself?

She gathered all these roses of sacrifice to be able to scatter them at his feet, and she never thought of asking for anything personal in return. She preferred to go to Jesus poor and empty handed, so that he would take pity on her misery.

Anything we do of ourselves lacks merit and, therefore, does not deserve any return, but if given to him and confided to his care it gains value from his divine merits and can be applied to the souls of others. Theresa never labored for herself. Her life's work was to obtain mercy for sinners.

The little Theresa who in the procession of the Blessed Sacrament tossed her flowers as high as she could to try to touch the monstrance, still continues to do so that they may reach the throne of God.

To give glory to God and his saints was always her chief joy. Now, since her entrance into heaven she continues to give glory to God and showers down roses upon many souls who seek her assistance.

Sister of Missionaries

Among souls dear to Theresa were the poor non-believers, immersed in the darkness of ignorance.

In spirit she visited their lands to sprinkle them with the redeeming blood of Jesus and to scatter over them her mystical roses.

She was very much interested in two young missionaries, and it came about in quite a simple way. While she was assistant to the mistress of novices, her one idea was to unite herself closer and closer to our Lord so as to be more help to the novices, and also to help missionaries whom she did not know but whom she admired and envied so much.

She had a special prayer: "Draw me to you, O Lord, and I will run to you," her idea being that the closer she got to God the more good she could do for others.

She said it was Jesus who inspired the prayer one morning after Holy Communion: "Draw me...and draw the souls I love."

A soul once captivated by the love of Jesus would no longer be able to live without his support. It is only natural that Theresa should desire to draw as many as possible to his Sacred Heart.

"As a torrent carries everything in its course to the open sea, so the soul that immerses itself in the vast ocean of

God's love, brings with it all its treasures." These treasures are the souls of those which God has brought in contact with her. For them she repeats the wonderful prayer of our Lord at the Last Supper.

Not only were her prayers answered for her brothers, but for many other souls as well, including those who "would have believed had they ever had a chance." The wonderful conversions that occurred after the death of St. Theresa attest to the efficacy of her prayers. Some were converted by the two missionaries she called her "brothers" and these converts further brought others to the Faith.

What a truly wonderful thing is the dogma of the Communion of the Saints!

Every virtuous act on our part finds its repercussion in the souls of others and helps in the work of their sanctification. A sinful act retards it or even renders it null and void. Therefore, how necessary it is for us to practice virtue.

It was in 1895 that Theresa was given her first spiritual brother. It was a washday and she was washing with all the ardor she put into all her works, when Mother Agnes of Jesus, then prioress, called her aside and read her a letter she had received from a young seminarian, who said he had been inspired by the great St. Teresa to ask for a Carmelite Sister who would be willing to consecrate herself to the good work of his salvation and for the conversion of the people among whom he would work.

Sister Theresa was overjoyed. It was what she had always desired and, in fact, longed for—a brother missionary.

This was Father Maurice Bellière of the White Fathers, then only a seminarian. He was twenty years of age, zealous and ardent for the evangelization of Africa, but sorely tried at the idea of having to leave his family and go into perpetual exile.

His first letter was dated October, 1895, and the poor seminarian was tormented in spirit with the thought of his early departure. He wrote to ask Sister Theresa to be a "mother" to him, especially since he had lost his own mother in infancy.

Sister Theresa replied: "Our divine Lord asks no sacrifice beyond our strength. At times, it is true, he makes us taste to the full the bitterness of the chalice he puts to our lips. And when he demands the sacrifice of all that is dearest on earth, it is impossible without a very special grace not to cry out as he did during his agony in the garden: *My Father, let this chalice pass from me!* But we must hasten to add: *Yet not as I will, but as you will.* It is so consoling to think that Jesus, *the strong God,* has felt all our weaknesses and shuddered at the sight of the bitter chalice—that very chalice he had so ardently desired.

"Your lot is indeed a beautiful one, since our Lord has chosen it for you, and has first touched with his own lips the cup which he holds out to yours.... Jesus treats you as a privileged child. It is his wish you should begin your mission even now, and save souls through the cross. Was it not by suffering and death that he ransomed the world? I know that you aspire to the happiness of laying down your life for him; but the martyrdom of the heart is not less fruitful than the shedding of blood, and this martyrdom is already yours. Have I not, then, good reason to say that your lot is a beautiful one—worthy of an apostle of Christ?"

Sister Theresa asked him then to recite the following prayer for her daily: "Merciful Father, I humbly ask you in the name of your only Son Jesus, and of the Blessed Virgin and all the saints to inflame the heart of my sister with the Holy Spirit of love, and grant her the grace of making others love you greatly."

"This spiritual communion for doing good to others, between a seminarian with a field of noble work before him," says Monsignor Lavielle, "and a soul aspiring after perfection, has something of the celestial about it."

Theresa in her letters to him often referred to her approaching death, and wrote to him: "You have promised to pray for me always, your life will certainly be longer than mine, and it is not yet given to you to sing with me, 'My exile, I hope, will now be short,' but, nevertheless, I hold you to your promise even if our Lord keeps his to take me soon. Continue saying that little prayer daily because, when in heaven, I shall still want what I desired so much on earth: to love Jesus and to make others love him.

"Perhaps you may think me strange and consider yourself illusioned to have a sister who wishes to leave you so soon to go and enjoy her eternal repose, leaving you to shoulder the burden of the work. But be comforted in the thought that all I desire is to do the will of God, and that if I felt that I could no longer work for his glory in paradise, I should choose exile rather than my heavenly home.

"I cannot see the future, but if in heaven Jesus permits my desires to come true, I promise I will always be a sister to you. Our relationship instead of coming to an end will weld itself closer than ever. Then there will be no more cloister, no dividing grilles, and my soul, free, will fly to your assistance in your lonely missions. Our roles will still be the same—to you the fighting with apostolic arms, to me prayer and love."

In a few words he let her see, or rather guess, the depth of his desire for his perfect union with God, and in this also she stimulated and encouraged him. "I, too, have thought the same as your director," she wrote to him. "You cannot be a saint by halves, you must give of your all. I saw from the first the generosity of your soul and that is why I was pleased to be a sister to you. Don't think you can alarm me by speaking of the years that you have wasted. No, on the contrary, I thank Jesus who has looked upon you with love, as he did upon the rich young man in the Gospel. You, more fortunate than he, responded to the call of the Divine Master, and you left everything to follow him, and this you did in the flower of your youth when eighteen years of age."

Not content with mere encouragement she spurred him on to greater heights in the acquiring of unlimited confidence.

"Oh! my brother," she wrote, "from the day on which it was given me to understand something of the love of the Sacred Heart of Jesus, I lost all fear. The remembrance of my faults humiliates me and leads me never to trust in my own strength, which is nothing but weakness, really, but he talks to me of nothing but love and mercy.

"How could our sins not be pardoned, if we with a trust similar to that of a child, throw ourselves into his arms repentant? We are then casting our sins in the furnace of his everlasting love where they will be consumed by the flames."

Her other "brother" was given to her by Mother Gonzaga in 1896. Adolph John Roulland, by name, was ordained a priest in that year and sent direct from the seminary to the foreign missions.

Before leaving France, and without any hope of returning, he wrote to Carmel through a friend, one of the Premonstratensian Fathers, begging to have one of the sisters help him with her prayers in his work for the missions.

On having his request granted, he went to celebrate Mass at the convent at Lisieux soon after his ordination, and both before and after the Holy Sacrifice he was granted a few words with Theresa.

God had indeed blessed this union of souls in a most particular manner six years previously. On September 8, 1890, Theresa, having that day made her profession, asked God to give her an apostolic soul, and if God would so grant it, one who would have her same aspirations and all her desires. As she herself could never be a priest, she wanted to be one by proxy. Now on that very day something happened in the soul of Adolph Roulland... what, exactly, we do not know, but he must have revealed it to St. Theresa because she wrote to him thus: "On September 8, 1890, your missionary vocation was saved by Mary, Queen of Apostles and Martyrs. On that day a little Carmelite nun became the spouse of the King of heaven. Her only aim in life was to save souls and, above all, souls of apostles, and so she asked Jesus to give her an apostolic soul to cooperate with. Not being able to be a priest herself she craved for one who would receive all the graces from our Savior and all the aspirations she would have had, had she been in his place.... You now know the unworthy Carmelite nun who made this prayer. Don't you think, then, as I do, that our spiritual union confirmed on the day of your ordination really began on September 8?

"I never thought I would meet the missionary brother this side of heaven, but the beloved Savior of humankind, lifting up a corner of the mystic veil that hides eternity's secrets, deigned to give me, while still in exile, the great consolation of knowing the brother of my soul and to work in collaboration with him for the salvation of souls."

The missionary departed for the district of SuTchuen, and there Theresa followed him in spirit. Before his departure she begged him to send up this prayer daily: "My God, permit Sister Theresa to gain souls for love of you."

She wrote to him on July 30, 1896: "I would that I could arrange that you should have all the consolations and that my share should be all the trials. Perhaps this is selfishness on my part, but I don't think so because my only weapons are suffering united with love."

And on March 19, 1897: "I should be so happy to work and suffer for a long time for Jesus, and I beg of him to do what he likes with me and not pay any attention to my desires either of wishing to suffer and love, or to go and join him in heaven.

"I hope that when my turn comes to leave this exile you will not forget your promise to pray for me, but I do not desire anyone to pray that I may be liberated from purgatory.

"St. Teresa of Avila used to say to her daughters, when they wished to pray for her: 'What does it matter to me if I remain in purgatory until the end of the world if at the end of that time I have managed to save one soul?' These words find an echo in my heart. I want to save souls and to forget myself in doing so. I wish to save them even after my death. Therefore I should be happy if instead of praying for me, you substitute the words: 'Please God, let my sister bring many souls to the love of you!'"

This correspondence of theirs ever remained supernatural and spiritual, but Sister Theresa foresaw that in some cases it might prove a source of danger, so on her deathbed she warned Mother Agnes: "Perhaps many young priests, hearing that I have been a spiritual sister to two missionaries, may write and ask for a similar favor and it might be a danger. Only by prayer and sacrifice can we be a help to the Church. Therefore, let this correspondence be a rare thing, and to some not permitted at all. They might be too much engrossed with it and imagine they are doing great things, whereas in reality, far from obtaining great graces, they would be opening the gates of the power of evil. Mother, what I say is very important. Do not forget my words when I am gone."

On the Wings of Love
and Suffering

"Many pages of this story," said Sister Theresa, "will only be read in heaven."

What this elect soul has let be known of her incessant immolation of herself to God was only a hundredth part of the sacrifices she offered up in the secret of her soul.

Her great ambition was to be a martyr. It was her most ardent desire, and she begged it from Jesus on the day of her profession—martyrdom of body and of heart. Her prayer was heard. She suffered always and greatly.

"Love," says G. Martin, talking of the Spiritual Little Way, "is born together with the germ of suffering. They are inseparable and grow side by side. It is impossible to love God without suffering." To begin with, it is suffering to those who love him, to see him so little cared for, and so often offended. It is painful to know that we ourselves do not really love him as much as we should, compared with our desires. It also causes suffering to feel one's limitations and one's inability to receive in a heart already overfull the immense waves of love and tenderness that come to it from the heart of God and almost inundate it.

There is another reason why a soul who ardently loves our Savior must also love suffering and be willing to accept sorrow and pain cheerfully: because this is the means for saving souls. To love Jesus is not sufficient for one who truly loves him. Theresa thirsted to gain souls for him at all cost, that they might love him for all eternity. She wished to save the worst sinners, but this can only be done by applying the infinite merits of the Redeemer to such souls. Only grace can save them, and this grace is the fruit of Calvary. It may reach them by mysterious ways, by a stream kept flowing by the voluntary sacrifices of a chosen few, who, with generous hearts, extend the sacrifice of the cross on their behalf.

Those whom Jesus Christ purchased by his death can only be saved by suffering. So we repeat, suffering is the inseparable companion of love.

Theresa's love had no bounds; neither had her suffering. If she invariably hid the latter with a smile, that does not detract from its merit.

In June, 1888, when they were fearing that her father would have another stroke, Theresa surprised her novice mistress by saying: "I am suffering a great deal, Mother, yet I feel I can suffer still more." She did not then see the trial that awaited her. One month after her vestition day, on February 12, 1889, her father drank deeply of the bitter chalice—he lost the use of his mental faculties. Theresa no longer said, "I could suffer more," and words cannot express her grief. There were three years of martyrdom for her father, of which she says: "They seem to me the sweetest and most fruitful of our lives."

This patient suffering alone would have been sufficient to proclaim her a saint, as her father was everything to her. She had concentrated all her affections on him, including those she had borne her dear mother, whom she had the misfortune to lose at such a tender age.

Theresa, we know, was very sensitive, but she was happy to be able to offer to God the various sufferings he was pleased to send her.

In a convent one's sensitivity is sharpened, but at the same time it is refined and one learns to bear things for the sake of love, though one's power of feeling is in no way diminished.

What a comfort it must be when knowing our dear ones are in trouble, to think of them under one's own roof. Theresa had two sisters, both Carmelites, in her convent, but not once since the dreadful news of her father did she seek consolation from them. Never did she, the youngest of them all, run to cry out her sorrow in their loving arms. It is so natural for one in pain to look for a grain of human comfort, to allow oneself the relief of tears and the feeling of despondency as a concession to nature. By neglecting a small rule as a result of the burden of sorrow, Theresa might have passed unnoticed under the circumstances. There was none of this for Theresa. The angels will testify that even in her overwhelming sorrow she never neglected her duties. The eye of God saw her heart and its grief, but to all around her she appeared the same as usual, sweet, attentive, willing, serene and obedient to the least of her duties.

She knew how to remain at the foot of the cross, strong and generous as always.

The only day she showed any emotion and shed any tears was on September 24. When she received the veil, her father was too ill to be present to bless his little Queen, and those tears were misunderstood.

While writing to Celine she was oppressed by grief and the hand that wielded the pen shook, but the words she wrote were a model of resignation.

"You know how much I counted on seeing our dearest father again. I see now that it is by God's will that he is absent from the feast. Jesus has sent us this trial to prove our faith and love. He wishes me to be an orphan so that I can be his alone, to unite myself more closely to him, and he will render to me in heaven the things he has denied me down here.

"The suffering of today is a pain difficult to understand. We had been looking forward to the natural and innocent pleasure of having dear father here on this great occasion. We awaited him with eager arms, but they have remained empty. This grief does not come to us from a human being but is sent to us by God. Celine, dear, let us join together in accepting this cross with a good heart. Our feast is turned into one of tears, but I feel that Jesus will be consoled by them."

How beautifully encouraging to us are the tears of the saints. They do not suffer any less because they suffer willingly. Their feelings are just as human as ours, perhaps even deeper. It is only their love that is greater.

For example, that sublime saint, St. Mary Magdalene de Pazzi cried and sobbed pitifully when she had seen her little brother in a vision in the flames of purgatory. It was pitiable to hear her moaning "my poor little one." How deeply she mourned her mother too, when the mother prioress came to break the news of her death.

Sister Theresa suffered also a great deal at the hands of the admirers of Mother Gonzaga, and one person in particular was bitter in her innuendoes with which she influenced nearly the whole community. Theresa described these as pains that made her suffer greatly. But she bore all patiently.

She also reveals that God gave her a bitter chalice to drink even in regard to her own sisters. She tells us no more, but even these few words give us food for thought. After all, she hadn't entered Carmel to live with her sisters. She could have done that at home, and she felt from the beginning that it might be a drawback instead of a help. She determined from the first day that she would treat them no differently than any of the others in the community, and this entailed many sacrifices on her part.

Mother Gonzaga used to say: "Sister Theresa is perfect. I have only one fault to find...she has three sisters in the convent."

Theresa informed her, however, that there was no real danger, because "We must forget our blood relationship and be sisters in religion only." She herself kept a strict guard over her own heart and never by word or deed showed them the extra, tender affection she had for them. This was a very difficult task which she had imposed upon herself. She had left home and family and would not go back on her sacrifice.

In the manuscript which she wrote in obedience to a command from the mother prioress she exclaimed on recalling these days: "Oh! my little Mother (Mother Agnes), how dreadfully I suffered at that time. I couldn't open my heart to you and I was afraid you would hardly know me."

Once when Mother Agnes was ill with bronchitis and her illness gave cause for some anxiety, Theresa was creeping gently along the corridor to replace the keys of the Communion grille and didn't want to awaken the patient, whom she was longing to see. She suddenly met one of the sisters who was full of zeal and energy and who, evidently thinking Sister Theresa would certainly make a noise and disturb the Reverend Mother, tried to take the keys from her. Theresa, young and inexperienced in those early days, argued that as she was sacristan the keys were in her charge and it was her duty to deliver them personally. This little whispered conversation did the very thing they both wished to avoid...the patient awoke and Theresa was blamed by the other sister. She made a great effort, however, in maintaining silence, and without excusing herself withdrew, realizing, as she said afterwards, that flight was better than running the risk of a losing battle.

She also said that during her novitiate she was constantly discovering new defects in herself and regretted them deeply. Later she avowed that she no longer became upset by them but rather gloried in her miseries and expected to find fresh weaknesses daily.

"I find more profit in being convinced of my absolute nothingness than studying the light of faith," she said.

At one time there was a question of sending Mother Agnes (her sister Pauline) and Sister Genevieve (Celine) to the Carmel of Saigon. Theresa felt as if her very heart would break at the thought of what her two beloved sisters would have to go through, but she never tried to dissuade them. But when the Carmel of Hanoi in Tonkin wrote and asked for Sister Theresa herself, she declared that she was ready to go into exile. She knew this would be a terrible wrench to her, but it was for that very reason, and the joyful thought of suffering greatly, that she wished to accept. In Lisieux she was known and loved, in Hanoi she was unknown.

"Many of the pages of my life will only be read in heaven," she wrote, and we think she must have been referring to all that she suffered through her affections and which she hid so well under a smile.

In Darkness

The martyrdom of her soul was certainly shorter, but far more dreadful than her physical sufferings.

From her earliest years, hearing her parents talk of eternity, relates Mother Agnes of Jesus, Theresa felt that the pleasures of this world were vain, indeed, when compared to heavenly bliss. Even when quite small she was convinced that she had no real dwelling place on earth, and that some day she would go far away to a land of happiness and perpetual light where she would have a fixed abode.

When she and Celine sat on the terrace at Les Buissonnets and gazed at the sky, they would try mentally to penetrate the veil of heaven. They never had any doubt as to the existence of their heavenly home.

Above faith they placed love, that love which later was to make them abandon everything of this world to follow him, who was the only one who could satisfy their hearts.

So great was their belief in the existence of heaven and a future life that it was impossible for them to conceive the existence of atheists and unbelievers. Then a terrible thing happened to Theresa herself in the year 1896, soon after Easter. All this profound conviction and sweet hope were swept away, and her mind was plunged into impenetrable darkness and unbelief! She seemed to hear a voice say-ing: "You dream of a land of light and fragrance, you dream that the Creator of these wonders will be yours forever, you think one day to escape from these mists where you now languish. Nay, rejoice in death, which will give you, not what you hope for, but a night darker still, the night of utter nothingness!"

Her finest poems were written during this time of dark-ness. She wrote not what she felt but what she believed.

Not one of her sisters in religion was aware of this mar-tyrdom of mind. They all thought that Theresa had fewer trials to contend with than any of them.

In her autobiography she wrote: "Dear Mother, this description of what I suffer is as far removed from reality as the first rough outline is from the model, but I fear that to write more would be to blaspheme...even now I may have said too much. May God forgive me! He knows that I try to live by faith, though it does not afford me the least consolation. I have made more acts of faith in the last year than during all the rest of my life."

She declared that not only the veil which obscured her faith had not been rent, but that a wall had sprung up as high as the heavens, hiding the light of the firmament. This wall was not removed until a short time before her death.

One night she was seized with a terrible feeling of an-guish, and confessed to Mother Agnes of Jesus, the moth-er prioress: "I was lost in darkness, and from out of it came an accursed voice: 'Are you certain that God loves you? Has he himself told you so? The opinion of creatures will not justify you in his sight.'" Mother Agnes' reassuring words comforted Theresa. She recalled the special graces Jesus had lavished upon her, and that she was dearly loved by God and that she was on the eve of receiving from his hands her eternal crown. Immediately peace and joy were restored to her soul.

She talked with Father Godfrey Madelaine one day. "To all outward appearance she showed nothing at all of these interior torments," he said, "and I asked her how she could hide her trials so successfully. She replied: 'I endeavor that no one shall suffer through me, so I keep these things hidden from all except the mother prioress and my confessor. With these two exceptions they are known only to God.'"

She gave no outward sign at all of this intense suffering, and to think that for a long time she endured the thought that she was to be eternally damned! Just for a moment she saw a ray of light in a dream that might have been called a vision.

In the early dawn of May 10, she thought she was walking through a subterranean passage with the mother prioress, not knowing how they got there. Suddenly, she perceived three Carmelites in mantles and long veils. She knew that they had come from heaven. "Ah!" she thought, "how glad I should be if I could but look on the face of one of these Carmelites!" Immediately the tallest of the three saints advanced toward her, and inexpressible joy took possession of her soul as the nun raised her veil and covered Theresa with it. Theresa recognized her as being the Venerable Mother Anne of Jesus, foundress of the French Carmel. She could not withdraw her gaze from that transcendently beautiful face, and notwithstanding the thick veil that was covering them both, Theresa saw the face of Mother Anne shining with effulgent light and her whole being seemed to radiate light.

The Venerable Mother lavished affection on Theresa, and the latter, seeing herself such an object of affection, dared to question her: "Mother, I implore you to tell me, will our Lord leave me down here much longer or will he come soon to take me?" "Yes, soon I promise you," was the reply. "Mother, tell me one more thing, I beg of you. Does our Lord want anything of me beyond my poor little actions and my desire to please him? Tell me if he is pleased with me."

The face of the Venerable Mother took on a fresh splendor and her expression was infinitely more tender and loving. "Our Lord," she replied, "does not require anything further of you, my child. He is pleased, very well pleased with you." And taking Theresa's head in her hands she kissed her with incomparable love and sweetness, such as Theresa was powerless to describe. She was overcome with joy, and when she suddenly thought of asking for some special grace for her sisters, unfortunately she woke up!

"O Jesus," she said, "you commanded the winds and the tempest, and a great calm arose." This dream strengthened her faith in heaven. Her joy, however, was of very short duration.

Darkness assailed her soul again—just at the time when both of her beloved sisters were thought to be leaving for Indo China at the bidding of Mother Gonzaga.

Sister Theresa had asked of our Lord to suffer martyrdom either of the spirit, or body, or both, if it would be his will. Her desire was granted.

The First Sign

As we have said, just a few days before the terrible darkness of her spirit was imposed on her, she had her first expectoration of blood, which made her aware that she was not long for this world.

She tells us about it with the most charming simplicity. On the evening of Holy Thursday she had sought permission to watch all night at the Repository, but it was not granted, and so at midnight she returned to her cell.

As soon as her head touched the pillow she felt a rush of something in her mouth and thought she must be dying. Her heart beat with joy at the very thought. As she had just turned out the light, she would not give way to curiosity by lighting it again, and out of mortification waited until morning to find out if her surmise were correct. With a tranquil mind she went to sleep.

This peace and tranquility of hers are surely heroic qualities under circumstances which to most people would prove alarming.

Even the strongest of us would feel a certain degree of fear at a sudden illness attacking when alone in the middle of the night.

Not so with Theresa. She rose at five o'clock as was her custom, but this time she was full of hope and joy, just as if she anticipated some very good news.

Drawing near the window to the light, she found her hope realized; her handkerchief was soaked with blood.

Her joy was great to think that her Beloved Spouse, on the anniversary of his own death, had given her the first clarion call which told her he would come before long and take her to himself.

She went to choir and recited Prime with extra fervor. Her happiness made her forget any sense of suffering or fatigue. She was longing to go and tell the mother prioress her precious secret and obtain her permission to finish the Lenten duties as she had begun them.

That same day Theresa used the discipline, continuing it during the recital of three Misereres. Toward evening, having had only a little bread and water all day, she stood on a tall ladder and began washing the large windows. A passing sister noticed her pallor and asked to take her place. Theresa wouldn't consent and kept on with her work until it was dark. Then she prayed and performed more penance.

When she returned to her cell, she "heard again the echo of last night's joy," which was her way of saying she had again coughed up blood. She had not deceived herself. She had always felt that she would die young.

In this added illness she kept her own counsel, so no one was aware of her condition, and she performed her usual duties as though nothing unusual was the matter with her. Even Mother Agnes had no suspicion of her illness. She was lamenting the fact to Sister Theresa in her last hours, but Theresa said, "Little Mother, don't fret. You would have been unhappy knowing I was ill and that nothing was being done for me."

Mother Gonzaga, a strong and robust person herself, could not in the least enter into the suffering of others, but in her defense let it be said that Theresa had given her the impression that her expectorations of blood were of no consequence. Theresa had a dry cough, which she couldn't very well conceal, and which should have revealed to anyone hearing it that there was something gravely wrong with her.

This continued all summer, and it grew worse in the autumn. The mother prioress felt anxious. She ordered a more strengthening diet for Sister Theresa, and the cough ceased for some time. Finally came the terrible winter of 1896. The paroxysms of coughing became more and more frequent, however, and of longer duration. Theresa was very glad that her cell was far removed from those of the other sisters, so that her cough disturbed no one.

Cold and shivering from having had to face the open cloister in snow or icy wind, she could scarcely reach her cell without collapsing. It would sometimes take her half an hour to regain her breath while holding on to the banisters. Her frozen fingers refused to do the work of undressing herself, and it then took her another hour of acute suffering before she got into bed...and such a bed! A hard pallet stuffed with straw was all she had to stretch her weary limbs on, and a couple of dark brown rough blankets did little to warm her.

Heroically did she try to fight the deadly fatigue and the awful weakness which caused her dizziness and made her feel faint. Still she struggled to be her usual serene self, telling herself to go forward with courage...ever forward.

A fever had also been undermining her health for two years, but not once did she ask to be relieved from doing any of her tasks, no matter how fatiguing they were.... At the Divine Office she felt at times that she must die on her feet if she had to stand a minute longer.

One of the novices began to notice how dreadfully ill Theresa really was and informed the mother prioress. Then they endeavored to restore her to health, but it was too late.

Theresa, so good, so grateful, speaks well of Mother Gonzaga's care of her then: "The care she lavished on me in my last illness has taught me a great deal about Christian charity. No remedy, however costly, is too expensive for her to try on me, and if it does not alleviate my sufferings she will try another with the utmost patience. When I go down to recreation she sees that I am so placed that no draft will come to do me harm."

From the known facts, however, it is clear that God permitted her illness to go on for a length of time before remedies at all were applied, and when they were, it was too late to cure her or to give her any relief.

For some time she continued occupying that distant, cold cell and she said: "I prefer to suffer alone, and from the moment I am taken much care of or sympathized with I don't feel happy anymore. I have arrived at the point where I am not able to suffer anymore, because suffering is now sweet to me, so do not worry on my account."

She had further expectorations of blood on July 6, 1897, and her life was in danger. The doctor diagnosed her condition as a severe attack of pneumonia, and noticing the discomfort of her cell and her hard bed, he ordered her placed in the infirmary.

Theresa loved her cell as a religious will love the place where she has fought her battles with self, practiced her virtues, and received divine graces. Hence she remarked on being moved, "I have suffered greatly there, but I should have been glad to die there."

Two days before, she had said something which gave them an inkling of her sufferings: "I read in the *Imitation of Christ* that our Lord in the Garden of Olives was enjoying all the delights of the Blessed Trinity, but his agony was none the less painful. It is a mystery, but I can assure you that I can understand it somewhat by what I am suffering."

Often painful remedies had to be applied. One day, af-

ter suffering from them more than usual, she was resting
during recreation, and overheard a sister who was in the
kitchen remark: "Sister Theresa will not live long, and
really sometimes I wonder what our Mother Prioress will
find to say about her when she dies. She will be sorely
puzzled, for this little sister, amiable as she is, has certainly never done anything worth speaking about."

Her nurse also heard the remark. Turning to Theresa,
she said: "If you relied upon the opinion of creatures you
would indeed be disillusioned today." "The opinion of
creatures!" she replied. "Happily God has given me the
grace to be absolutely indifferent to that. Let me tell you
something which showed me, once and for all, how much
it is worth. A few days after my clothing, I went to our dear
Mother's room, and one of the sisters who happened to be
there said on seeing me: 'Dear Mother, this novice certainly
does you credit. How well she looks! I hope she may be
able to observe the Rule for many years to come.' I was
feeling decidedly pleased at this compliment when another
sister came in, and looking at me, said: 'Poor little Sister
Theresa, how very tired you seem! You quite alarm me. If
you do not improve, I am afraid you will not be able to
keep the Rule very long!' I was then only sixteen, but this
little incident made such an impression on me, that I never again set store on the varying opinion of creatures."

On another occasion someone remarked: "It is said that
you have never suffered much." She smiled very sweetly,
and pointing to a glass which contained medicine of a
bright red color, said: "You see this little glass? One would
suppose that it contained a most delicious draft, whereas,
in reality, it is more bitter than anything else I take. It is
the image of my life. To others it has been all rose color.
They have thought that I continually drank of a most delicious wine, yet to me it has been full of bitterness. I say
bitterness, and yet my life has not been a bitter one, for I

have learned to find my joy and my sweetness in all that is bitter."

"You are suffering very much just now, are you not?" her novices asked. "Yes, but then I have so longed to suffer.... I have reached a point where I can no longer suffer, because all suffering is become so sweet...."

"I Will Let Fall
a Shower of Roses"

Poor Theresa, how much she suffered! Each time the doctor came, he could barely conceal his admiration for her, and remarked: "If only you knew what she has to endure! I have never seen anyone suffer so intensely with such a look of supernatural joy.... I shall not be able to cure her. She was not made for this earth."

She still retained her charming simplicity and when they praised her for her patience, she would say: "Don't you understand even yet, that it is not my patience but our Lord's! Minute by minute he gives the little dose of it that is necessary. Just at this minute I feel I cannot go on enduring it any longer, but I am sure that if my pain were to increase our Lord would immediately increase the strength necessary for me to bear it."

She admitted she did not dare ask for more suffering "because that would be mine, and I have never in life been able to do anything on my own."

When someone asked her how she managed not to give way to discouragement, she replied: "I turn to God and all his saints, and thank them notwithstanding. I believe they want to see how far my trust may extend. But the words of Job have not entered my heart in vain: *Even if God should*

167

kill me, I would still trust in him. I own it has taken a long
time to arrive at this degree of self-abandonment, but I
have reached it now, and it is the Lord himself who has
brought me there....

"I do not fear the last struggle, nor any pains—however great—my illness may bring. God has always been my
help. He has led me by the hand from my earliest childhood, and on him I rely. My agony may reach the furthest
limits, but I am convinced he will never forsake me."

Theresa needed so much courage too. All food nause-
ated her and at three o'clock every afternoon she ran a very
high temperature. She would expectorate blood two or
three times daily. Her state was such that no remedy
seemed of any avail. Her face retained much of its beauty, but her body was reduced to a mere skeleton.

The tuberculosis had degenerated into gangrene, and
Theresa used the words applying to Christ: "I am a worm,
not a human being."

She was parched with thirst, according to her: "just as
if I were in purgatory" and nothing was able to quench it.
In fact, whatever she drank seemed to have the contrary
effect, causing a burning sensation.

In an effort to relieve her terrible spells of coughing, they
propped Theresa up in bed with pillows, but she felt as if
she were sitting on two pointed red hot irons and begged
to be allowed to lie down, asking them kindly to pray for
her. She had to undergo all this without any real hope of
heaven's assistance, for the impenetrable darkness of her
soul was still enveloping her.

Her two martyrdoms, that of body and soul, were fused
into one, nailing her to the cross with Christ. Our Savior
asked of her the sacrifice of everything, for now even the
reception of Holy Communion was denied her.

From August 16 to September 24, the vomiting was
continuous.

Theresa had long before asked Jesus to remain in her heart from one Communion to another and for always. She knew that Jesus dwells in a soul that is in the state of grace. We do not know if it was a miracle she asked for, that is, the actual presence of our Savior as when received in Holy Communion. We can well believe that Jesus might have performed this miracle for one who cherished in her heart her living God, as he is preserved in the ciborium.

On August 6, the feast of the Transfiguration, they placed by the side of Theresa's bed a picture of the Holy Face surrounded with flowers, and set in front of it a small vigil light. That night was for her the worst of all. The temptations against faith were more terrible than before.

"Oh! my Mother," she said to her sister, "how desperately I am tempted tonight. I have not dared to take my eyes off the Holy Face and I've never ceased making acts of Faith.

"Mother, pray for me, I beseech you. If you only knew what I suffer.... Pray that my patience may endure. I have so much need of God's help. I yearned to suffer every kind of martyrdom, yet one must go through some of it oneself before one can realize what it means.

"I can almost understand how the poor wretches who have no faith put an end to themselves when they have come to the end of their endurance.

"If you should have any in your care who suffer atrociously, do not leave any poison near them, because, Mother, when one suffers like this it would take only an instant to lose one's reason and the deed would be done.

"What happiness it is to me to feel I am nearly at the end now," she continued. "I wish I could tell the others what transports of joy I have in my soul, but that would be of little encouragement to them, if they thought I hadn't suffered greatly.... If you only knew what I am suffering!... Tonight, as I feel, I cannot bear much more. I have asked our Blessed Lady to take my head in her hands to help me to endure to the end.

"My soul [here Theresa pointed to a dark alley in the garden] is like that black spot, but I am walking there in peace."

Ill and suffering as she was, she nevertheless still managed to smile and keep her sweet serenity toward all who approached her, and many came each day, because they all wanted to see her and hear her speak.

"In spite of everything," Mother Agnes says, "she always remained little, and her soul retained its peace and tranquility.

"She confided in me so many of her dearest hopes and desires, and longed that they would very soon be realized."

"Like St. Joan of Arc in prison, I am now in fetters, but soon the time of my liberation will come, and that will be the time of my conquests.

"When I am suffering greatly and something very painful and unwelcome happens to me, I always meet it with a smile instead of putting on a mournful air. At first it wasn't at all easy but now it has become a habit and I am very happy to have acquired it!"

In this very painful and protracted illness, in which she had endured no less from the drastic remedies employed than from the disease itself, lying there on her bed of suffering she again heard two of the sisters discussing her in a very disparaging manner. One of them remarked: "When all is said and done I don't think she could even be called a very good religious."

A smile broke on Theresa's face, and later she could not resist telling one of the other sisters, a very saintly woman, about it, adding: "Can you imagine what a joy it is to me to be told on my deathbed that I am not even a good religious?" The recipient of the confidence, speaking of it later said: "I don't know when I have felt as edified over anything as over Sister Theresa's deep and sincere humility. She knew she had nothing, and was nothing. All her strength, all her riches and her salvation came to her from the Infinite Mercy of God."

Vastly different was God's attitude toward her. Heaven seemed in a state of suspense waiting for the last beat of that heart that had pulsed only for God, and the last breath of that pure and innocent victim who had opened her heart to the flames of Divine Love.

Only a little while longer and she would be consumed by that fire.

On the night of June 4, Sister Theresa looked as if she were transfigured and no longer suffering. To the sisters who were in her cell, she said: "I am so very happy, dear Sisters, I am dying fast. Do not be surprised if I do not appear to you after my death, and you receive no signs of my great felicity. You must remember that this is my little way, not to wish for anything of that kind. I have so often spoken to you of this, telling you that I should not be seeing you down here.

"I should like for your sakes, however, to have a beautiful death.

"Do not grieve if you see me suffer much at the end. You may not see any sign of happiness in me, either, when I leave you, but remember, our Lord was a victim of love, and consider what his agony was.

"I do not know if I shall go to purgatory, but if I should have to, I will never regret not having asked to be spared its torments just as I shall never regret having worked solely for the salvation of souls. I heard with great happiness that our Mother St. Teresa worked also for the same end." Torn as she was between love and suffering, she began to speak prophetically of her mission in heaven.

"I have never given the good God anything but love! It

is with love he will repay. *After my death I will let fall a shower of roses.*"

On another occasion when one of the sisters was speaking to her of the happiness of heaven, Theresa interrupted with these sublime words: "It is not that which attracts me."

"And what attracts you?" asked the other.

"Oh! It is love! To love, to be loved, and *to return to earth to win love for our Love!*"

"Mother!" she said, "some notes from a concert far away have just reached my ears, and have made me think that soon I shall be listening to the wondrous melodies of Paradise. The thought, however, gave me but a moment's joy—one hope alone makes my heart beat fast: the Love that I shall receive and the Love I shall be able to give!"

On July 16, the feast of Our Lady of Mount Carmel, Theresa received the Anointing of the Sick at the hands of a newly ordained priest, who said his first Mass in their chapel that morning. From the chapel to Theresa's cell the cloisters and corridors were strewn with rose petals and wild flowers, and the temporary altar in the infirmary was also decorated with a profusion of flowers. Marie Guerin, whose name in religion was Sister Marie of the Eucharist, at Theresa's request, sang a hymn in her beautiful, melodious voice, the words having been written by Theresa herself.

Most surprising of all was Theresa's consciousness of the mission for which our Lord had destined her. On more than one occasion she revealed the secrets of the future, which have since been realized.

"I feel that my mission is soon to begin," she said, "my mission to make others love God as I love him...to teach souls my *little way. I will spend my heaven doing good upon earth.* Nor is this impossible, since from the very heart of the Beatific Vision the angels keep watch over us.

"No, there can be no rest for me until the end of the world. But when the angel shall have said: 'Time is no more!' then I shall rest. Then I shall be able to rejoice, because the number of the elect will be complete."

"And what is this *little way* that you would teach souls?"

"*It is the way of spiritual childhood, the way of trust and absolute self-surrender.*

"I want to point out to them the means that I have always found so perfectly successful, to tell them that there is but one thing to do here below. We must offer Jesus *the flowers of little sacrifices* and win him by a caress. That is how I have won him, and that is why I shall be made so welcome.... We can never have too much confidence in the good God; he is so mighty, so merciful. As we hope in him, so shall we receive."

Not only to the pure, good and innocent souls does Theresa point out her little way, but to everyone, including the greatest sinners. If one has committed mortal sins, that is no reason for doubting God's infinite mercy, and one should never lose complete trust in him. With a heart broken with sorrow and repentance, the sinner should fall at the feet of his Savior, recalling how he loved the prodigal son, recalling his words to Mary Magdalen, and the woman taken in adultery, as well as to the Samaritan woman at the well, knowing full well that Jesus' love and mercy will never fail if we ask for them. All those sins would disappear in a moment like water thrown into a furnace, if we only approach him with love.

To prove her words she related a little anecdote taken from the life of one of the Fathers of the desert.

One of the Father's converts, a woman who had been a public sinner and a scandal to the country, touched by divine grace followed the saint into the desert to perform rigorous penance. On the first night of their journey into the desert and before they had reached the place of retreat her love and grief and repentance were so great that her heart was broken and she died. At that very moment the saintly Father saw her soul, in a vision, being carried up to heaven. "There," said Theresa, "you have a striking example of what I wish to convey to you, but these things are often difficult to explain."

She would have loved to have been able to inculcate these thoughts into the minds of sinners, as she wished so much to lead them all to Jesus and leave them safely in his embrace. Daily she was growing feebler. The doctor remarked: "No one could wish to prolong her life, seeing how terribly she suffers. But she bears it all like an angel, never complaining and always smiling."

Last Words

Being now so very near death she took a tender leave of all those dear to her.

For her own sister Carmelites she copied a charming letter written by Blessed Theophane Venard, the angelic martyr whom she so much resembled, and to whom she felt drawn because of his great love for Mary Immaculate.

"My soul is so like his," she wrote to Leonie as well as to one of her brother missionaries and her Uncle Guerin.

To Father Roulland she wrote: "I announce to you with joy my proximate entry into the Holy City. What I look forward to more than anything in heaven is the hope of at last being able to love God as I have always desired and the thought that I may be able to influence people to love him and praise him for all eternity.

"On the point of my being called before him to give an account of myself, I see that only one thing is necessary: to work solely for God and not for oneself or creatures. Jesus wants the whole of our hearts and for this one must go through a lot of suffering, but on her entry into heaven what an immense joy will flood the heart of one who has given up all for him!

"I am not dying; I am entering into life...and from the height of heaven I will be better able to make you understand what is so difficult to say clearly to you down here."

To Abbot Belliere: "Isn't the greatest treasure of all Jesus? Well, he is in heaven. Therefore, it is there your heart should dwell. This gentle and merciful Savior has long ago forgotten your faults and he now only considers your efforts in striving toward perfection, and that rejoices his heart. I implore you do not remain dejectedly at his feet, but with a gesture of pure love throw yourself into his arms. That is the place for you. I am more than ever convinced of it since reading your last letter. You must not travel to heaven by any other road than the one your sister has taken.

"When you read these few lines I shall perhaps be no more. I know not the future, yet I can confidently say that my Spouse is at the door. It would take a miracle to keep me in exile, and I do not think Jesus will work that miracle—he does not because I shall be free from suffering, on the contrary, suffering combined with love seems the one thing worthy of desire in this vale of tears. But I am happy to die because, far more than on earth, I shall help the souls I hold dear.

"When my brother departs for Africa I will follow him not only with my thoughts and prayers, but I will be near him always. His faith will teach him to find this faithful companion, the little Carmelite sister whom Jesus has given him to be a help not merely for two years or so but for all eternity.

"These ideas may seem to you a little fantastic but, remember, Jesus has always treated me as a spoiled child...."

A few days previously her sisters had asked her: "Will you look down on us from heaven?" "No, I will come down," she replied. "I think of all the good I can do to others after my death...I shall see that babies won't die without Baptism...and I want to help all missionaries and the whole Church."

The poor missionary who was given her for a spiritual brother was very sad when he learned of her severe illness and certain death. He had counted on her constant help for many years. She wrote to him again: "I feel we must tread the same road to heaven—the road of suffering and love. When I have reached the port, I will teach you how best to sail the world's tempestuous sea—with the self-abandonment of a child well aware of a father's love, and of his vigilance in the hour of danger.

"I long so much to make you understand the expectant love of the Heart of Jesus. Your last letter made my own heart thrill sweetly. I learned how closely your soul is sister to mine, since God calls that soul to mount to himself by the *elevator of love*, without climbing the steep stairway of fear. I am not surprised you find it hard to be familiar with Jesus—one cannot become so in a day. But this I do know, I shall help you much more to tread this beautiful path when I lay aside the burden of this perishable body. Ere long you will exclaim with St. Augustine: 'Love is my lodestone!'"

Right up to the moment of her death, her solicitude was for the missionaries.

According to a promise she made to the mother prioress she went for a very little walk daily in the garden before being confined to bed. Pale, feeble and drawn she would totter, leaning heavily on her stick. She looked like a walking shadow, and a sister passing by remarked: "Sister Theresa, you would do much better to rest; walking like this cannot do you any good. You only tire yourself!" "That is true," she replied, "but, do you know what gives me strength? I offer each step for some missionary. I think that possibly, over there, far away, one of them is weary and tired in his apostolic labors, and to lessen his fatigue I offer mine to the good God."

A letter from her Uncle Guerin at this time is enchanting in its affectionate simplicity, and his answer is so beautiful that it is quoted here in full.

"My dear little Angel:

"Your letter was a delightful surprise and its unfeigned cheerfulness brought us comfort, but made me weep at the same time. I cannot explain my tears because they were caused by a multitude of feelings, my pride for instance, for having such an adopted daughter, my admiration for her great courage and her love for God, and...I cannot hide it, dear love...an infinite sadness impossible to disguise when faced with a separation that seems to be an eternal one. Faith and reason protest, and we give in to their arguments, but they do little to mitigate our sorrow.... You were always the little pearl, recently left to us by your dear mother. You were the 'little Queen' of your aged father. You were the most beautiful flower in that wreath of lilies that crowns me and gives me a foretaste of celestial bliss.

"My suffering at the idea of losing you has been great, and I have almost wished to wrest you from your heavenly Spouse, who is now calling you.... They say that the swan, a silent and dumb bird all his life, sings a beautiful song at the approach of death. Your letter, my love, is certainly your swan song, and it brings with its sorrowful news, the saintly thoughts destined to help us through this time of great grief, and perhaps to share a few of the sparks from that divine furnace of love by which you are looking forward to being completely absorbed.

"Dear little privileged soul, even in your tender infancy you saw the burning bush and were so fascinated by its glow that you approached so near as to be absorbed into its flames.

"Farewell, dear child of mine, precious pearl confided to my care by your mother. The remembrance of your virtues and your innocence will never leave me, and I hope that your prayers will obtain for me the grace of being one day reunited with all my dear ones in our eternal home.

"He who, perhaps, has a certain right to call himself your second father, embraces you with all the love of his heart."

Isadore Guerin

The little saint was deeply moved upon reading these tender, loving words.

It was a last look on all that was dear to her on earth, and she recalled the tenderness always lavished on her.

From that moment, quietly and simply, she turned all her thoughts to her last end.

A Glorious Death

"I think I have often been afraid of death," she said, "but I have never been afraid of what would happen after death.

"Only one thing I ask myself: What can this mysterious separation of soul from body really be? It was the first time I had really put the thought into words, but I immediately put myself in the hands of God and asked for the crucifix, and said, 'Let me kiss it and gain the plenary indulgence in favor of the souls in purgatory. It is the only thing I can do for them.'" On September 14th they brought her a rose. She began to strip off its petals, wiping the wounds of our Lord on the crucifix with each in turn. The petals fell, one by one, on the floor and she said: "Pick them up, they will give pleasure to someone some day." The sisters obeyed and not only did the petals give pleasure, but many and singular graces were obtained through them.

With surprising calm she made all her last depositions to her "little Mother."

"I am like a very tiny child, and sometimes I do not think of anything at all, unless it is to unite myself to God and conform myself entirely to his holy will, suffering from moment to moment whatever he chooses to send me without any thought of the future. I don't even rejoice at the thought of death because it is merely the expression of God's will for me. I desire neither death nor life. I only will what he wills. It is what he does that I love."

When breath began to fail her she moaned: "I suffer, I suffer," but later she said to her nurse: "When I say, I suffer, please add for me: 'So much the better' because that would really be the completion of my sentence, but so often I haven't the strength to say it."

After September 25, she was unable to move, and could scarcely say a single word without suffering intense pain.

One of her last pleasures was the visits of a little robin redbreast that loved to play around her bed, pirouetting and chirping.

At 9 o'clock one evening a dove alighted on her window sill uttering her plaintive little cry. Both Celine and the invalid recalled the verse in the Canticle: "The voice of the turtledove is heard; arise my dove, my beloved one and come because the winter is over."

Her last hours were thus described by her dearly loved sister, Mother Agnes of Jesus:

"On September 27, a novice in the infirmary, struck with Sister Theresa's fortitude under terrible pain, said to her, 'You are an angel of patience and meekness.'

"'Oh! no, I'm not an angel,' she replied. 'Angels cannot suffer, they cannot be as happy as I am!'

"September 28. 'There is a lack of air. I cannot breathe. When will God let me breathe the pure air of heaven?'

"September 29. The day preceding her death: she seemed to be in agony from early morning, and had to struggle for each breath.

"After the doctor's visit she asked: 'Mother, will it be today?' The answer was in the affirmative: 'Today our Lord is very well pleased.' 'And so am I,' courageously added Theresa. 'If I could only die now, how happy I should be!'

"The office and prayers of St. Michael the Archangel were recited, then the prayers for the dying. When the passage relating to demons was reached she made a childlike gesture smiling: 'I am not afraid.'

"In the afternoon: 'I can scarcely bear it. Let them pray for me. If you only knew....'

"Sister Genevieve (Celine) asked for a word of farewell. 'I have said all.... *All is consummated!* Only love counts.'"

After Matins, while undergoing a real martyrdom of suffering, she joined her hands and with a low, sad voice murmured: "Yes, my God; yes, my God; yes, I want it all...."

"Are your sufferings very terrible?" asked Mother Prioress. "No, dear Mother, not so terrible, but it's just as much as I can bear; no more, no less."

She asked to be left alone during the night, but the mother prioress would not consent to this. Sister Marie of the Sacred Heart and Sister Genevieve of the Holy Face shared the night in watching, and they were happy not to leave her.

The morning of September 30, she was awakened during Mass. She didn't speak; her exhaustion was too great, and she was breathless. Her suffering must have been beyond words.

Suddenly she clasped her hands and looking up at the statue of our Blessed Mother said: "Oh! with what fervor I have prayed to her.... And yet it has been pure agony, without a ray of consolation.... Earth's air is failing me: when shall I breathe the air of heaven?"

One can say that her last night on earth was one of excruciating suffering. For several weeks she had been unable to raise herself in bed, but at half-past two in the afternoon, she sat up and exclaimed: "Dear Mother, the chalice is full to overflowing! I could never have believed that it were possible to suffer so intensely.... I can only explain it by my extreme desire to save souls...." And shortly after: "Yes, all that I have written about my thirst for suffering is really true! I do not regret having surrendered myself to Love."

After repeating these last words several times, she added: "Mother, prepare me to die well." The mother prioress encouraged her with these words: "My child, you are quite ready to appear before God, for you have always understood the virtue of humility." Then Theresa bore witness to herself in these striking words:

"Yes, I feel it; my soul has ever sought the truth.... I have understood humility of heart!"

The agony of this "Victim of Divine Love" began at half-past four. From that moment it did not seem as if she could be suffering. Rather, like the martyrs of old when given over to their executioners, she seemed to be sustained by a divine force.

The community gathered around her, and she thanked them with the sweetest smile. With her crucifix clasped in her weak hands, she entered into the final combat. Her brow was heavily laden with the sweat of death. She was not dismayed, because her soul was strong in faith, and she could see the beacon-lights of heaven. Like a pilot, when close to harbor after a furious storm, she valiantly put forth every effort to reach the shore.

At six o'clock, hearing the Angelus bell, she raised her eyes to the statue of our Lady, the Star of the Sea.

Shortly after seven o'clock Theresa asked: "Mother, is it not the agony?... Am I not going to die?" "Yes, my child, it is the agony, but Jesus perhaps wills that it be prolonged for some hours."

Theresa was resigned to the will of God, and in a sweet and plaintive voice, replied: "Ah, very well then...very well...I do not wish to suffer less!"

Then, Theresa looking at her crucifix, said: "Oh!...I love him!... My God, I...love...you!"

These were her last words. Scarcely had she uttered them when, to the surprise of all, she sank down suddenly, her head inclined a little to the right, to await the summons of her Divine Lover.

All the sisters knelt around her bed and were witnesses of the ecstasy of Theresa's last moments.

Quite suddenly Theresa raised herself, and opening her eyes, fixed her gaze slightly above the statue of our Lady. Immediately after this ecstasy, which lasted about the space of a *Credo,* her blessed soul was borne away to heaven.

This was about 7:20 P.M., September 30, 1897.

Our beloved little saint preserved in death all her youthful beauty and her sweet smile.

She was clutching her crucifix so tightly that it was with difficulty removed when she was prepared for burial.

Sister Marie of the Sacred Heart and her companion fulfilled this sad office with the assistance of Sister Anne of Jesus, the infirmarian.

All three noticed that Theresa did not look a day older than thirteen or fourteen years of age. Her body remained flexible until the day of burial, which took place on October 4, 1897.

Two other things were noticed on the evening of September 30:

During Theresa's very long agony a number of little birds congregated on a tree just outside her open window, and they sang and sang until the very moment she died. Never had there been such a concert in the garden before. It seemed so joyous, and as the community was so sad the contrast was great.

One of the sisters who had rather misunderstood Theresa in life was surprised and touched by it, and drew our attention to what had already been observed.

During her illness, Theresa had predicted that when she would die the weather would be fine. Whereas the entire day of September 30 had been dull, gloomy and rainy, toward seven o'clock the clouds disappeared and the stars began to shine.

The Reason
for an Autobiography

Instead of the usual circular letter which is sent to all the convents of the Order on the decease of one of its members (and containing a brief summary of the nun's life) in October, 1898, all the Carmelite convents received *The Story of a Soul*, that is, the autobiography of Sister Theresa of the Child Jesus.

Many will ask why the autobiography was written, considering it is not usual for a Carmelite nun to write her own life. But small and insignificant things which appear in our eyes to have happened quite casually are, on the contrary, often born in eternity because they are in the mind and the will of God. They are like sparks that eventually cause a fire, germs of a plant that know not death... and so it was in this case.

In 1894, on a December evening, Mother Agnes, then prioress, Sister Marie of the Sacred Heart and Theresa were seated around the fire in the community room. The presence of the mother prioress enabled them to talk a little on the past events of their lives. Theresa, who still had the gracious ingenuousness of a child, narrated many family episodes of her youth, which enabled both of her sisters to recall many happy and sad memories.

Sister Marie of the Sacred Heart took the mother prioress aside, and asked her: "Don't you think it is rather a pity that Sister Theresa, who is so gifted with her pen, should be writing poetry for different sisters and not leave us a record of her infancy and childhood? Our dear little sister is, I feel, not long for this world. She is too much of an angel to be left here, and afterwards, when we no longer have her among us, we shall be sorry not to be able to recall so many beautiful memories that would be of interest to others as well as to ourselves."

The mother prioress considered the matter for several weeks. Then she sent for Theresa and told her to write all she could remember of her life from earliest infancy, and to let her have it for her feast day.

Always a model of obedience, Theresa set herself to the task without question, early in 1895, giving only a few odd moments to it daily when her work as sacristan allowed her the leisure. In January of the following year she had it ready. At the evening prayer on January 20, she passed in front of the stall of the mother prioress, genuflected, and placed the book before her. It was well written, neat, and without erasures. It was penned on very poor paper.

Mother Agnes didn't reply or look at her. She simply inclined her head to show she acknowledged it. Making an act of mortification which hurt her just as much as it did her sister, she delayed reading it for several months, until someone replaced her as mother prioress and she had more leisure. In all those months Theresa never gave a thought to her manuscript, especially as her "little Mother" had informed her it was still unread. She put it entirely out of her mind.

When Mother Agnes did eventually read it, what joy and edification it gave! She marveled at the operation of grace in the soul of her little sister from the very dawn of the age of reason. What an immense amount of good would be done to souls by its perusal! She felt she would like the memoirs to be more complete, but as she was no longer prioress she couldn't give orders. Should she mention it to Mother Gonzaga who was so authoritative and wedded to tradition?

Days passed. Sister Theresa's health was failing, and still Mother Agnes hesitated. Finally on June 2, 1897, she interviewed the mother prioress and succeeded so well in persuading her, that the order was given to Theresa to continue the work and complete it.

"I had already prepared a copy book for her," says Mother Agnes, "but she thought it too good and was afraid of sinning against holy poverty. She asked if I didn't consider it better to write very small and closely so as not to use too much paper. I told her she was too ill to tire herself unnecessarily, and that she was to write it large and clearly."

"Well, what am I to write about?" she asked Mother Agnes before beginning. "Write about charity and about the novices," she replied, and Theresa did as she was told.

"I write about charity," she said, "but I cannot do it as I would wish. In fact, I don't think it could be worse. There is no consecutiveness in it, but perhaps my meaning may be understood all the same."

Sister Theresa was really too ill then to undertake the work. She wrote about fifty additional pages, in the same clear hand and with no erasures—then one day in the beginning of July the pen fell from her hand.

She wrote those few pages in the garden in the shade of the chestnut trees, in an old wheelchair which had been used by her father in his last illness. She was constantly interrupted in her work by one or another of the novices, who often came to seek her advice.

The last words were written in pencil, because she was so weak she hadn't the strength to keep on dipping her pen in the ink (fountain pens had not yet come into use).

One would never guess on seeing that firm, clear hand-writing, and reading the spontaneous freshness of the manuscript, that it was written by one so young and so near death. Even when she writes of her own illness she did so with utmost simplicity and without exaggeration.

The manuscript was divided into three parts: the first part, comprising eight chapters, was written for Mother Agnes; the second, containing the ninth and tenth chapters, for Mother Gonzaga; the third, which consists of one chapter, the eleventh, was written for Sister Marie of the Sacred Heart, who in September, 1896, asked her to write a memorandum of what she called her "little way."

"Dear Sister," she said, "you have begged me, by way of a souvenir, for a description of what I have called my 'little way.' As soon as I get permission from the mother prioress to write it, I will begin, as it will be a great plea-sure for me to converse with you who are my sister twice over."

"What would you do," asked Mother Agnes, "if the Mother Prioress were to cast your manuscript in the fire?"

"Well, I shouldn't have any doubts about my mission. I should simply think that God would find other means of granting my desires."

This idea of hers of fulfilling a mission after her death was mentioned by her more than once during her lifetime, and more especially during her last illness.

When, for example, Mother Agnes made known her plan to read Theresa's manuscript aloud to the commu-nity and later perhaps to have it published, even if it might displease some people, Theresa said: "Mother, after my death no one must know of this book until it is actually published. If you were to talk about it, the devil would most certainly put a spoke in the wheel and try and inter-fere with God's plan, which is a *most important work*."

Another time Mother Agnes asked her to reread a part of the manuscript, because it seemed to lack something. Returning to the infirmary later she found Sister Theresa in tears. "What! Crying?" she asked. "These pages are so moving to me.... Yes, I feel they will do a lot of good. One can learn from them some of God's goodness and mercy. I feel those who read my words will love me...," and so it has turned out to be.

Mother Gonzaga was profoundly impressed by Sister Theresa's last agony. During the few months which elapsed after the saint's death a great change came over her. She became gentler, and her benevolence grew with her humility. Her remembrance of Sister Theresa was one of gratitude and veneration.

Facing a portrait of Theresa Mother Gonzaga obtained a wonderful grace, known only to herself, and from that day she could never look at the picture without weeping. She told Sister Genevieve of the Holy Face: "I am the only one who knows what I owe her. If you only knew what she said to me, and oh! so sweetly."

In fact, the night before Mother Gonzaga died, in 1904, full of saintly humility, thinking of the judgment of God, she said in a deeply humble voice: "Notwithstanding my faults, and because I have Sister Theresa to intercede for me, I am certain that I shall owe my salvation to her prayers."

With the complete change of character, wrought through the influence of Theresa, it had been easy to persuade Mother Gonzaga to have the book published.

The Very Reverend Father Gonzaga Madelaine, then Prior of the Premonstratensians of Mondaye, was charged with the reading of the manuscripts. It was he who presented it to Bishop Hugonin to obtain the Imprimatur. The letter of approval was given on March 8, 1898, and in October the book was distributed to the various Carmelite convents, arousing a great deal of enthusiasm.

Meanwhile, the *Story of a Soul* passed from the Carmelite convents to friends of the Carmelites, and it wasn't long before it was being read by thousands. At the end of World War I the *Story of a Soul* had gone forth to all lands, having been translated into thirty-five different languages.

In France alone 410,000 copies were sold of the full-sized life and 2,000,000 of the abbreviated one; 30,388,000 of her portraits and numerous relics were distributed. This in itself is a miracle.

Never did a book have such a sale! It has been read and admired by Popes, by the learned and the ignorant, by believers and unbelievers, by Catholics and non-Christians.

His Holiness, Pius XI, called it "The Marvelous Book," and on the very day of Theresa's canonization he expressed his views in these words: "The book written by Sister Theresa about her own life, in the pure beauty of her mother tongue, describing her spiritual infancy, is not only a book for everyone to read, but it penetrates by its sweetness into the hearts of the most hardened of men, some of them very far indeed from Christian perfection. A good many of them have been converted by reading it and are keeping themselves in the charity of Christ."

"I Seek Only the Glory of God"

The 20th of August, 1914, saw the death of the saintly Pontiff, Pius X. He died of grief over the outbreak of one of the most inhuman wars the world has ever seen, which neither his voice nor his fatherly heart had been able to prevent.

One of the last acts of his reign was to sign the decree introducing the cause of our saint, whose name was already known throughout the world.

Declared a wonder-worker from the first by the voice of the people, she had shown that through her intercession both bodies and souls were cured. She obtained many conversions, splendid vocations, and extraordinary help for priests, missionaries and nuns.

The graces were often prodigious. A wonderful favor was granted in 1906 at the Seminary of Bayeux. During recreation one day the young seminarians were discussing Sister Theresa of the Child Jesus: some loud in her praise, others lacking in enthusiasm. One most vociferous in praise of her was the seminarian Anne, a native of Lisieux, who later was well rewarded for his faith in her. In 1904 his iron constitution began to show signs of failing. Acute hemorrhages denoted tubercular trouble in an advanced stage. Both lungs were very badly affected. He continually ran a high fever and suffered from great repugnance to all food. The doctors pronounced it galloping consumption, and said he could not live long.

Someone placed a relic of Sister Theresa around his neck, and a novena was begun for his cure, but he grew alarmingly worse.

One night the infirmarian suggested that he offer up the sacrifice of his life, since she never thought he could live through the night; but the young man didn't in the least want to die and would not give up hope. He said he felt that Sister Theresa was near him and that her wish was to give him back to the Church and to his family.

Holding the relic to his heart, he exclaimed, "Oh, dear little Sister Theresa, I feel sure you are in heaven, and I am down here where there is so much good that needs to be done. You *must* cure me!" He felt a confidence in her intercession such as he had never had before. Immediately he sat up in bed. Pain, exhaustion, want of breath and fever had all disappeared in an instant.

Indeed, it was a complete cure. The doctors were obliged to declare a supernatural intervention. The lungs were entirely healed and showed no trace of the former disease.

Later Abbot Anne became chaplain of the Central Hospital in Lisieux, where he had eight hundred people in his charge.

On February 10, 1910, Monsignor Lemonnier, Bishop of Bayeux and Lisieux, received permission from the Sacred Congregation of Rites to proceed with the Cause for Theresa's beatification. The informative process on the life and virtues of the servant of God began in August of that year and closed in December, 1911.

Exactly a year later, the Sacred Congregation sent forth the decree of approbation on account of the writings of the saint, and His Holiness Pius X signed the introduction of the cause to the Roman Court.

On her deathbed Sister Theresa told the sisters that they

would not find her body incorrupt. She had always wished everything about her to be very simple and normal and had prayed for nothing out of the common for herself. The first exhumation in September, 1910, revealed only her bones; but the palm that had been placed at her feet in the coffin was as green and as fresh as on the day of her burial, and from the coffin arose a most exquisite perfume of roses, which the very earth around the grave seemed to exhale.

During World War I, Sister Theresa was seen by many on the battlefield and in the trenches. She was mother, sister, Angel of the French, Italian, German and English soldiers. While she was present, hatred seemed to disappear, and each nation in turn invoked her aid. She comforted those in their agony, reanimating their flagging courage, and led many back to God.

Airplanes, too, were named in her honor. Whole regiments were consecrated to her and the French soldiers named her their second guardian angel.

What could be more touching than the prayer of a young subaltern going into the front line: "Oh! Sister Theresa of the Child Jesus, protect me as a mother would, for my mother isn't here!"

An aviator wrote: "I am in despair as I have lost my relic of Sister Theresa."

A trooper writing to his mother stated: "As soon as I received the little souvenir of Sister Theresa I was filled with joy and I had no more fear."

From trenches and camps came innumerable letters from soldiers begging for her beatification.

Theresa is still showering roses everywhere.

The mother prioress received a letter on April 23, 1911, from a Presbyterian minister living in Edinburgh, saying:

"More than a year ago a book came to my notice. It was a translation into English of an autobiography of Sister Theresa of the Child Jesus. I opened it disinterestedly and my attention was immediately captured by the beauty and originality of the ideas. I considered that the work of a genius had fallen into my hands, with the thoughts of a theologian, and the mind of a poet.

"I suddenly felt that difficult-to-express feeling, when one is aware of a supernatural presence, and said to myself: 'Theresa is here, in this room.' Her saintly face was so imprinted on my memory that I could not lose sight of it, and she seemed to be saying to me: 'That is how Catholic saints love Christ. Listen to me; choose my "little way." It is the only sure one, because it is the only true one.'

"I then began to invoke her aid with a joy that I can scarcely describe. Then one day she said to me: 'Why do you beg me to pray for you, if you won't know and invoke our Blessed Lady?'

"I saw at once that it was illogical of me to invoke St. Theresa and ignore the Mother of God. It was like a blinding light to me. I turned at once to the Blessed Virgin. I was surprised by the immediate response I received. My soul was flooded with a new and great love, and it is a love that goes on growing daily and is now immeasurable."

The Reverend Mr. Grant made his submission to the Church on April 20, 1911, and received conditional Baptism. His life became very difficult for him in the town where he had practiced as a clergyman of the Free Scotch Unitarian Church, so he and his wife (also a convert) went to France. They made their home at Alençon, in the very house where St. Theresa was born, and he and his wife entertained the many pilgrims who came to visit the home of the saint. He died there in sanctity on July 19, 1917.

While the Apostolic Process went on in Lisieux a new and extraordinary miracle happened with signs of incontrovertible authenticity. It did much to strengthen the favorable opinion of the judges in Theresa's favor.

It was with regard to a nun of the teaching order of the

Congregation of the Daughters of the Cross, Sister Louis of St. Germaine, who had suffered from 1912 with a duodenal ulcer which caused terrible hemorrhages. She was in a deplorable condition in 1915 and received the last sacraments. She no longer asked Sister Theresa for the prolongation of her life. She only asked that she obtain for her a holy death. But she didn't die.

At the beginning of September, 1916, a sister passing from one convent to another reanimated her faith and persuaded her to pray again for a cure. In the middle of the night between December 10 and 11, the saint appeared to her and said: "Be generous; you will soon be cured, I promise." Then she disappeared.

The following morning the nurses were astounded to find on the floor all around the bed rose petals of all colors: a certain sign that St. Theresa had been there, and a still more certain sign that the patient would be cured. But from then until December 21, she grew very much worse; in fact, she was near death. It was a great test of faith that was asked of her.

On the night of December 21, she placidly went to sleep. The following morning she awoke completely cured.

On August 14, 1921, His Holiness, Benedict XV signed the decree declaring Sister Theresa's virtues heroic.

On February 11, 1923, His Holiness, Pius XI signed the decree of approbation of the miracles. Therefore, March 26, 1923, was a day of rejoicing for the little town of Lisieux. The few people who in October, 1897, had followed that modest little coffin in the precincts of the convent certainly must have thought that chaste little body would remain there until the day of judgment. They would hardly have believed it if they had been told that the humble remains of that little nun would in a few years be removed with great pomp and ceremony in the presence of a large concourse of people.

After fulfilling the legal verifications, the coffin was placed on a magnificent white hearse adorned with rich brocades, and drawn by four white horses in glittering harness. It was escorted by three hundred priests, all the religious communities of Lisieux, about twenty Catholic delegations and a group of officers of various regiments, including a guard of honor from the American Army in full military dress with flags flying, commanded by Captain Huffer, Vice-Commander of the American Legion from Paris.

No music, no bands; only the Rosary and the psalms from the Common of Virgins were recited. Everything breathed of reverence and prayer. A lady who was present asked for the conversion of her husband, and soon had the joy of seeing him approach the sacraments after thirty years of lapsed Catholicity.

A wounded war veteran gained the use of his legs.

A lady from Paris was cured of an internal disease.

A poor working man who was unable to use his right arm as a result of many operations, regained the use of it and was able to return to work and support his family.

A blind woman asked for the gift of sight. Her request was granted and the precious relics of St. Theresa were the first things she saw.

When the coffin passed into the little Carmel Chapel where Theresa had prayed as a child, as a young girl, and as a nun, a magnificent new organ sounded a triumphal march, after which the hymn, "Jesu Corona Virginum," was sung. The bishop then gave a last and Solemn Blessing. The crowd gradually departed and Sister Theresa's remains, surrounded with flowers, were left at the foot of the altar.

The pilgrims dispersed quietly and wended their way to the station, where seven special trains conveyed them to all parts of France.

Many lingered to pray at the gate of the chapel. Some were still there until the early hours of the morning. One wonders what must have been the feelings of the saint's own sisters during this triumphal procession; still more, what they must have thought when Monsignor Lemonnier, holding the skull of the saint in his hands, carried it inside the cloister to be venerated by the entire community; and later when, with the cloister door open, all the sisters garbed in their white mantles and carrying lighted candles came to meet the sacred relics, just as a few years previously they had come to greet Theresa at the age of fifteen as she entered Carmel to serve God by love and suffering.

Thus did her sisters Marie, Pauline and Celine come to do homage to their own little sister and venerate her relics.

Blessed

Sister Theresa was beatified on April 29, 1923. In St. Peter's on that occasion there were present forty-five bishops, all the ambassadors appointed to the Holy See, a great number of Prelates and thousands of the laity.

After the reading of the Brief of Beatification, Monsignor Lemonnier intoned the "Te Deum." Then the basilica blazed into light and in the "Gloria of Bernini," a portrait of the saint was illuminated with countless lights. The multitude was swaying with enthusiasm. During the solemn Mass hundreds of priests gathered in the choir and made the responses with the Bishop of Bayeux: "O Lord, who hast said, 'Unless you become as a little child, you shall not enter into the kingdom of God,' grant us, we beseech you, to faithfully follow the blessed virgin Theresa in her way of humility and simplicity of heart, so as to merit one day a part in her eternal reward."

When the Mass was over the crowd slowly left and many people, soldiers, magistrates and high dignitaries of the Church were seen unashamedly wiping their eyes, saying: "What a beautiful function!"

In the afternoon Pius XI descended into St. Peter's to do homage to the new "Beata," an unusual procedure, reserved for canonized saints. The tones of the big bells announcing Theresa's triumph seemed to resound throughout the world. Thousands of bells echoed and reechoed in Rome, from the ringing of the big Cathedral bells down to the tiny tinkle of the Missionary Church: it was a glorious hymn to the new saint.

The triduum at Lisieux had taken place a little before the one at Rome. Notwithstanding the presence of His Eminence Cardinal Vico, Legate of His Holiness; of the Primate of Normandy, and of the Bishops of Treves and Evreaux, the smallness of the Carmelite Church gave the impression that it was a private ceremony.

A far more imposing ceremony took place later in the Cathedral of Lisieux. Three Cardinals were present: Cardinal Bourne, Primate of England; Cardinal Dougherty, Archbishop of Philadelphia, Pennsylvania, U.S.A.; Cardinal Touchet, Bishop of Orleans, France; and fifteen other bishops. The preacher on the last evening was Cardinal Touchet.

What did the Eagle have to say about the Dove?

He, the Bishop of Orleans, had come to pay a debt of gratitude to the "Beata." The Eagle fixed his eyes on his six thousand listeners, and beginning to speak, took his flight to the sublime heights of spiritual rhetoric, but first he told them that when the procedure for the canonization of St. Joan of Arc suddenly came to a standstill, he implored the aid of Sister Theresa of the Child Jesus, and shortly after that Pope Pius X revoked his former decision and hastened the exaltation of the *"Pucelle d'Orleans."*

The Cardinal extolled Theresa's powerful intercession with God, and showed how this power is due to her incomparable love—a love so ardent, tireless and generous that it caused the All-Highest to bend to this humble daughter of his heart, affording her a wonderful intimacy with him. He reminded them of her role of consoler to the soldiers in the war. Then addressing the Cardinals from foreign lands he entreated them to proclaim far and wide in their own countries that France had a horror of war and only sought a just and lasting peace.

Since they were honoring the little saint of peace and love, it was fitting to close with this thought of peace. As the Cardinal ended his talk he was warmly applauded.

The festivities came to an end in the evening with a procession in which Theresa's relics were carried through the streets. Later, it was acknowledged that many miracles had occurred during the procession.

Saint

On the occasion of the canonization of a saint, the devil, envious of all good, trembles with rage and senselessly pits himself against the new saint. His rage is for the numberless souls the saint wrests from his grasp and gives to God.

There is nothing so foolish, however, as this rage of his, because the first to canonize a saint is God, the Eternal Truth. The Church merely ratifies on earth what has already taken place in heaven.

"Theresa's glory is ever on the increase," said the Assistant General of a large congregation, when speaking of the long list of wonderful graces obtained through her intercession. "Yet," he added, "we are far from having reached the summit. This little saint who works such wonders in our times is only showing us a glimpse of the resplendent glory which will be hers in the kingdom of God, when she will have her palm in her hand for all eternity."

Daily, new miracles were reported to the Sacred Congregation from all parts of the world. Multitudes requested the canonization of Sister Theresa, and public acclaim triumphed in the end.

The great day was fixed for May 17, 1925, and innumerable people thronged St. Peter's for this happy occasion. Thirty-four Cardinals, more than two hundred archbishops and bishops, numerous prelates, and thousands of religious of various orders preceded the *Sedia Gestatoria* in the grand procession.

The face of the Pope was radiant.

The unheard-of triumph of the one he called his second guardian angel, the advocate of the interests nearest his heart, was also a triumph for him.

Fifty thousand faithful thronged the immense Basilica. The Cardinals, Patriarchs, Primates, Archbishops, Bishops and Abbots passed in front of the Holy Father and paid him homage. First came the customary postulations and the invocations to the Holy Spirit. Then the Secretary of Briefs said: "Rise. Peter will now speak through the mouth of Pius." A profound silence came upon the crowd.

In that majestic silence Pius XI pronounced the formula that led up to the great "Hosanna." The Pope had spoken. From the cupola came the sound of the silver trumpets as if heaven itself were joining in the solemn acclamation.

The gift of miracles that God bestows upon some of his elect is proof that it is his will they should be honored. When the Church, adoring this holy will, encircles the brow of a holy person with the halo of sanctity, all who are loyal to the Church's teaching authority should bow their heads and believe.

The bells of St. Peter's filled the air with their deep tones and in response all the bells in Rome rang out the joyful news, until the very air was filled with the joyful sound.

The Holy Father then intoned the "Te Deum," which was followed by the *Oremus* to the saint.

The Pope then celebrated Mass. After the Gospel he gave a beautiful resume of the life of the new saint. Like his predecessor, he praised Theresa's "little way," and exhorted all the faithful to imitate it.

The great day closed at Lisieux with a magnificent procession. A chest containing the relics of Saint Theresa was carried by some Carmelite Fathers, followed by a military escort. Banners of forty nations were prominent in the procession, giving evidence of the homage paid the "Little Flower" by the whole world.

It was a wonderful sight, even from an artistic point of view, to witness the lengthy procession wending its way through the public gardens under the shade of century-old trees. The blaze of color from the vivid scarlet robes of the Cardinals and the purple and crimson of those of the bishops, in contrast with the white of the Carmelite cloaks and the gold on the beautiful vestments left an impression on all present which no one could ever forget.

Father Martin gave a brief address. Afterwards the *Credo* was sung by thousands with a fervor that made it quite evident that their religious enthusiasm had been deeply stirred, that they were willing with God's grace to follow St. Theresa of the Child Jesus in her "little way" of spiritual childhood.

After this the procession returned to the Carmelite Convent.

The whole town was illuminated that night. The chapel of Carmel was flooded with light, and the star that surmounted the cupola recalled Pius XI and his "dear star."

The star was over the cross: by sorrow and suffering St. Theresa had risen to glory and from the cross to eternal light.

"Il Carmelo," a Roman publication, said, "St. Theresa of the Child Jesus in her 'little way' has shortened space."

She barely tasted life; she flew on the wings of sanctity by prayers, mortification, and love; and with lightning speed traveled the road to eternal glory.

Novena to the Most Holy Trinity

To Obtain Graces Through
the Intercession of St. Theresa

O Eternal Father, who art in heaven, where you crown the merits of those who in this life serve you faithfully, for the sake of the most pure love your little daughter, St. Theresa of the Child Jesus, had for you, so as to bind you to give her whatever she desires, listen to the petitions which she offers up to you on my behalf, and hear my prayers by granting me the grace I ask.

Our Father, Hail Mary, Glory.

Prayer—O little St. Theresa of the Child Jesus, who during your short life on earth became a mirror of angelic purity, of love as strong as death, and of wholehearted abandonment to God, now that you rejoice in the reward of your virtues, have pity on me as I leave all things in your hands. Make my troubles your own—speak a word for me to our Lady Immaculate, whose flower of special love you were, to that Queen of Heaven "who smiled on you at the dawn of life." Ask her as the Queen of the Heart of Jesus to obtain for me by her powerful intercession, the grace I yearn for so ardently at this moment. Ask her also to give me a blessing that may strengthen me during life. Defend me at the hour of death, and lead me straight on to a happy eternity.

Hail Holy Queen.

Prayer for Missionaries to St. Theresa

St. Theresa of the Child Jesus, you who have been rightly proclaimed the Patroness of Catholic Missions throughout the world, remember the burning desire which you had here on earth to plant the cross of Christ on every shore and to preach the Gospel even to the consummation of the world; we implore you, according to your promise, to assist all priests and missionaries and the whole Church of God.

SP St. Paul Book & Media Centers:

Alexandria, VA
Anchorage, AK
Boston, MA
Charleston, SC
Chicago, IL
Cleveland, OH
Dedham, MA
Edison, NJ
Honolulu, HI
Los Angeles, CA
Miami, FL
New Orleans, LA
New York, NY
King of Prussia, PA
San Antonio, TX
San Diego, CA
San Francisco, CA
St. Louis, MO
Staten Island, NY
Toronto, Ontario, CANADA